ALL ABOUT KING ARTHUR

Arthur was certainly not invented by the
Normans, nor by the Anglo-Saxons whom
the Normans subdued. Whoever he was, he
came from farther back still. So does a great
deal of his legendary setting. The Anglo-
Saxons themselves were descended from a
conquering race—their ancestors had
invaded and settled in Britain from about
A.D. 450 onward—and Arthur was thought
of as a king of the Britons who possessed
the country before they overran it. Arthur
belongs somewhere in what is now called the
Dark Age, after the Romans, but before such
Anglo-Saxon sovereigns as Alfred.

Pictures, maps and archaeological
discoveries in this book help to piece
together the facts behind King Arthur and
his legend.

3cde

Other ALL ABOUT BOOKS

ALL ABOUT FOOTBALL
ALL ABOUT MONEY
ALL ABOUT WEATHER

and published by CAROUSEL BOOKS.

All About King Arthur

Geoffrey Ashe

CAROUSEL EDITOR: ANNE WOOD

CAROUSEL BOOKS
A DIVISION OF TRANSWORLD PUBLISHERS LTD
A NATIONAL GENERAL COMPANY

ALL ABOUT KING ARTHUR

A CAROUSEL BOOK 0 552 54039 0

Originally published in Great Britain
by W. H. Allen & Co. Ltd.

PRINTING HISTORY

W. H. Allen edition published 1969
Carousel edition published 1973
Reprinted 1973

Copyright © Geoffrey Ashe, 1969

Carousel Books are published by Transworld Publishers Ltd.,
Cavendish House, 57–59 Uxbridge Road, Ealing, London W.5.

Filmset in Photon Times 12 on 13 pt. by
Richard Clay (The Chaucer Press), Ltd., Bungay, Suffolk
and printed in Great Britain by
Fletcher & Son, Ltd., Norwich

CONTENTS

PHOTOGRAPH ACKNOWLEDGEMENTS

British Museum pictures appear by courtesy of The Trustees of the British Museum; other illustrations by courtesy of:

Edwin Smith
Charles Woolf, M.P.S.
Radio Times Hulton Picture Library
The Mansell Collection
National Library of Scotland
National Museum of Antiquities, Scotland
Bibliothèque Royale, Brussels
Aerofilms Ltd.
J. K. St. Joseph—Cambridge University Collection
Leslie Alcock
Bodleian Library, Oxford
John R. Freeman & Co. Ltd.
H. J. P. Arnold
City of Liverpool Museum
J. A. Coulthard—City Museum, Sheffield
Warner Bros.—Seven Arts
National Portrait Gallery
Sydney W. Newbery
G. J. Bakker

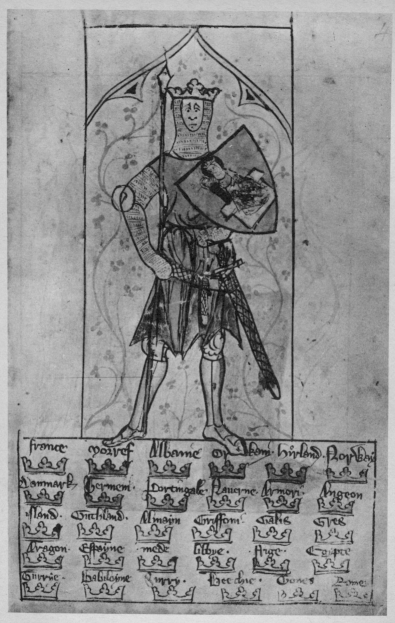

King Arthur, with crowns representing countries supposed to have been under his rule. (13TH CENTURY MANUSCRIPT—BRITISH MUSEUM)

INTRODUCTION

ARTHUR, KING OF BRITAIN, became a national hero between the years 1150 and 1200. The real ruler during most of that time was Henry II. But the legendary monarch was soon more widely renowned than the actual one ... and his fame in romance has continued ever since.

While King Henry was struggling with enemies on all sides, and in danger of going under, this was the sort of thing that was being written about King Arthur:

What place is there within the bounds of the empire of Christendom to which the winged praise of Arthur the Briton has not extended? ... The eastern peoples speak of him as do the western, though separated by the breadth of the whole earth. Egypt speaks of him, and the Bosphorus is not silent. Rome, queen of cities, sings his deeds, and his wars are not unknown to her former rival Carthage. Antioch, Armenia and Palestine celebrate his feats.

Asians, perhaps, were not really quite as much impressed as this author makes out. But right on through the Middle Ages, a long series of story-tellers kept Arthur glowing in the imagination of Europe. A vast public knew him: the most glorious of British kings, with his queen Guinevere, his city

Camelot, his Knights of the Round Table—Sir Lancelot, Sir Tristram, Sir Galahad, and the rest—and Merlin the wizard, and the ladies Iseult and Elaine.

But was there ever any such person? And if so, when?

We can think about him in two ways. Some people find the first more interesting, some prefer the second, some like to try both. We can ask what the 'Arthurian Legend' is, and how it started. What exactly are these stories that have been loved so long and told so often? Who told them first, and when and where? Or we can probe behind the Legend and look for facts. Did Arthur and his knights ever exist? How far are the stories true, how far are they invented? If any of the things happened, when did they happen?

In this book we shall explore both paths. But if you care for only one of them you can skip the chapters that deal with the other, without missing very much that is likely to interest you.

1

THE 'MATTER OF BRITAIN' AND HOW IT GREW

THE PEOPLE WHO MADE THE Legend fashionable under Henry II lived mostly in the castles of England and France. In those days the households of noblemen were becoming more cultured, more gracious, after a long age when barbarism was the rule. The Crusades had opened up trade with the East. New tastes, new luxuries, new ideas and interests were spreading everywhere. Another great change was happening too. With so many of the men away in the Holy Land for years at a time, women had become more important. They had learnt how to run things and to make their voices heard.

One result was that castles and manor-houses were providing an ever larger, more lively-minded audience for entertainers—for minstrels who sang and played, for story-tellers who kept the household amused during long dark evenings. And among the audience, besides men with wider knowledge and interests than their fathers, there were usually several keen-witted women. Sitting in the torchlit hall, they worked with their needles and spinning-wheels as always. But they were less afraid to speak up, and they wanted to hear more than the rough ballads of warfare and sport which had satisfied their own fathers.

Most of the stories that were composed to meet the chang-

11

ing demand were in verse. A poet would often know his work well enough to recite it from memory. As there was no printing, whatever was written down had to be written slowly by hand. Books were scarce and high-priced. Even the rich could not always read. So when a popular story was copied out in a book it was still generally meant to be read aloud. The clerk who did the copying might add little pictures, knowing that these would be welcome, if the book was handed round, to people who could not make much sense of the text.

Story-telling was a different art then in other ways. A modern novelist normally invents his plot for himself. We do, of course, have historical and biblical novels, which are woven round events of the past or themes from Scripture. But whereas, today, such books belong to a special class, in the Middle Ages nearly all serious story-telling was like this. The poets seldom made up their own plots or the main characters. Mostly they drew their themes from ready-made sources—collections of well-known legends and traditions that had taken shape in earlier times—even though they added and altered freely. As soon as a poet began to speak, as soon as a manuscript was opened, the listener or reader knew roughly where he was and what to expect, like a modern reader who takes up a novel based on the Bible such as *Ben Hur* or *The Robe*.

The three chief sources of themes for story-telling were called the 'Matter of France', the 'Matter of Rome', and the 'Matter of Britain'.

The 'Matter of France' meant a collection of tales about Charlemagne and his peers, headed by Roland, and their wars against the Saracens. Everybody knew that Charlemagne was a real person, the mighty ruler of France and neighbouring countries around the year A.D. 800. The

French kings claimed to be his heirs. Hence, the epics which told how he saved Christendom gave the French crown a special dignity. They were enjoyed by the warlike nobles who owed allegiance to it. But they were not so well suited to the taste of other countries, or to the fast-changing audience of the later twelfth century.

The 'Matter of Rome' covered everything that had come down from the ancient Romans, and from the Greeks also. This included Roman history and poetry, which were preserved in ancient books copied out by the monks. It also included Greek mythology. Western Europe knew less about this, because most of the Greek manuscripts were far away in the Balkans, Constantinople, and the Near East. Few westerners could have read them, anyhow. But stories like the Trojan War and the Voyage of the Argonauts were fairly familiar. So were the pagan gods, under their Latin names, such as Jupiter and Venus.

The 'Matter of Britain' meant the legendary history of Britain, which was growing more and more popular after about 1150 as a rival source to the others. Here is where King Arthur came in. By far the best loved of the British legends were those that dealt with Arthur and his brave company of knights. To most foreigners who took any interest in such topics, medieval England was the land of King Arthur, and Arthur was what they were apt to think of when England was mentioned.

Yet he wasn't 'history' as Charlemagne was history. Nor was he 'mythology' as, say, Jason was mythology. So what was he? And what exactly was the 'Matter of Britain', and where had it come from?

Arthur was certainly not invented by the Normans who ruled England after William the Conqueror, nor by the

Arthur's father Uther consults Merlin at Tintagel, with Ygerne in the background. (13TH CENTURY MANUSCRIPT—BRITISH MUSEUM)

Anglo-Saxons whom the Normans subdued. Whoever he was, he came from farther back still. So did a great deal of his legendary setting. The Anglo-Saxons themselves were descended from a conquering race—their ancestors had invaded and settled in Britain from about A.D. 450 onward —and Arthur was thought of as a king of the Britons who possessed the country before they overran it. As the Anglo-Saxon conquest took hundreds of years, this did not date him very precisely. He belonged somewhere in what is now called the Dark Age, after the Romans, but before such Anglo-Saxon sovereigns as Alfred.

The conquered Britons' descendants lived on, especially in Wales and Cornwall, and across the Channel, where many had settled (hence the name Brittany). For centuries no one else took much notice of them. But they were not completely crushed or silent. They made a comeback. Partly through travelling minstrels, their poems and traditions began to be known outside—in England, France, even Italy. And early in the twelfth century a British King Arthur began to attract interest because he kept getting mentioned. Sometimes very strangely.

In 1113, for instance, a party of French priests visited Bodmin in Cornwall. They had holy relics with them. A Cornishman with a withered arm asked for their prayers, hoping that the relics would do his arm good. They chatted together, and the Cornishman told them of the British hero King Arthur, who had lived in Cornwall in distant times and fought the Saxons . . . and was still alive. The priests laughed at this. They were startled to find that the townspeople backed him up. A fight broke out. The crowd took a good deal of pacifying, and the arm got no better.

Twelve years later, William of Malmesbury, a learned monk, was writing a history of England. To do research he went to Glastonbury Abbey in Somerset, a monastery so ancient that its real founder was unknown. Christianity was said to have been brought there in Roman days. A small church in the grounds was supposed to have been built by disciples of Christ himself. Whether or not there was anything in these tales, Glastonbury Abbey certainly did go back to the age when the Britons still held Somerset.

William heard British traditions handed down by the Glastonbury monks. He had already been told fairy-stories of Arthur, like the Bodmin one, which he didn't believe. But at Glastonbury he began to get a picture he could accept. Arthur, it seemed, was a Briton who took command against the Anglo-Saxon invaders, and pushed them back for a while, winning a crushing victory at a place which the Britons called Mount Badon. All sorts of wild legends had gathered round him since. Yet he did exist. So William concluded, anyhow.

William's research was helped and encouraged by one of the royal family, Earl Robert of Gloucester. Robert had friends in Wales, and he was interested in their proud ancestral traditions. Now he helped some other scholars to collect more and write them down. It was a member of this group, Geoffrey of Monmouth, who launched the 'Matter of Britain' and put King Arthur on the map as a figure of historic stature.

Geoffrey was at least partly Welsh himself. His father's name was Arthur, so perhaps, as a boy, he heard more than most about the hero from whom his name was taken. At any rate, between 1135 and 1140 he wrote a book in Latin entitled *The History of the Kings of Britain.*

The *History* is one of the most important books of the whole Middle Ages. Also it is one of the most puzzling. Geoffrey says in a preface that he got most of it from a much

Arthur rides into Camelot. (14TH CENTURY MANUSCRIPT—BRITISH MUSEUM)

older book in the British language—which could mean either Welsh or Breton. There is no doubt that he did know many legends, poems, and so forth, passed down from the misty age when Arthur was supposed to have flourished ... and from still earlier times. But that ancient British book of his has never been found. All too probably he only pretended to have it, and made up most of *The History of the Kings of Britain* himself.

It is not history. Not the sort you can trust.

Geoffrey begins in the world of Greek and Roman mythology. He tells how some refugees from the fall of Troy found their way to Britain and named the island after their leader, Brutus, who became its first king. After Brutus there is a long line of kings descended from him. Among them are

Lud, founder of London, and Lear and Cymbeline, the same who appear in Shakespeare. By the time Geoffrey comes to Cymbeline, who actually did reign over part of Britain in the first century A.D., he is getting into genuine history and cannot invent quite so freely. But he tries to make out that Britain was never a Roman province. His line of kings goes on. The Romans are only their overlords or protectors, in a vague sense.

The *History* starts moving towards its climax in the fifth century. Britain has a rightful king named Constantine followed by an usurper named Vortigern. So far no Angles or Saxons have come to Britain. They are living in heathen savagery on the opposite side of the North Sea. But Vortigern makes friends with the Saxon chief Hengist, invites him to settle in Kent with many followers, and marries his daughter Rowena. The Saxons revolt and treacherously murder most of the British nobles. A large part of the country falls into their power.

Two sons of Constantine, Ambrosius and Uther Pendragon, restore the true royal house. The wizard Merlin comes on the scene. Among other feats, he uses magic to transport an ancient stone monument across the sea from Ireland to Salisbury Plain . . . which is how Stonehenge got there. Merlin aids Uther in a love affair with Ygerne, a West Country lady. Arthur is their son. He is born at Tintagel Castle on the north coast of Cornwall.

At last Geoffrey reaches the reign of Arthur himself, making it the most glorious of all. Arthur succeeds to the throne while very young, but soon shows his mettle by a brilliant campaign against the Saxons in Britain, who are forced to submit. He bears a sword called Caliburn, forged in the enchanted island of Avalon, and he routs the enemy at Bath, which is where Geoffrey locates the mysterious Badon of tradition.

King Arthur marries a lady of Roman family. Geoffrey calls her Ganhumara, but we know her better as Guinevere. Then he conquers some countries overseas, including Ireland, Iceland, Norway, and France. He holds court at Caerleon-upon-Usk in Monmouthshire. Some of the romantic 'Camelot' setting is already sketched in Geoffrey's story, but some is not. Arthur has no Round Table. However, he does preside over a gallant band of knights. Several of the well-known figures are here, such as Bedevere, Kay, and Gawain. Others have not yet made their entry. There is no Sir Lancelot in Geoffrey of Monmouth's book, no Galahad, no Tristram. Nor is there a Holy Grail. The knights never ride out alone on quests or adventures like the knights of later romance. They are too busy fighting in their king's many wars. To win the love of ladies, they are not expected to slay giants or dragons, but to show courage in battle.

They have no choice. Arthur's Britain is strong and prosperous, but Geoffrey does not let him enjoy his triumphs in peace. While he is abroad fighting Lucius, an imaginary Roman ruler, his nephew Modred revolts. Britain is torn by civil war. Arthur is gravely wounded at the battle of Camlann, fought in Cornwall in the year 542. However, he does not die. Or at least, his death is not described. Geoffrey leaves the door open for the folklore belief about the King being still alive—the belief which the French priests heard at Bodmin. We are simply told that Arthur was taken away to Avalon for his wounds to be healed. After him, the Britons went on quarrelling among themselves and sinning in other ways, and the Saxons conquered them. But sooner or later, they—that is, their descendants in Wales, Cornwall, and so on—will recover and be on top once more.

So said Geoffrey of Monmouth. As time passed he added to the *History*, and wrote further of Merlin and Arthur's last voyage to Avalon, portrayed as an island paradise in the Atlantic. Its name means the 'place of apples'.

Geoffrey's book was written during the reign of Stephen. England was ravaged by civil war at the time, and the book did not succeed overnight. There was no printing then, of course, so the copying of books was a slow process. But gradually Geoffrey's story found a public. By the time peace returned, it was widely known and widely believed. It was a readable story in days when readable stories were still rare. Not enough true history had been written to expose its unlikeliness. Also it gave a framework to fit other stories into. The medley of British legends and ballads which had been floating about in the west and spreading eastward could now be put together and seen as a whole—just like the mythology of Greece and Rome, or the saga of Charlemagne.

And this was the original 'Matter of Britain'. This was what story-tellers drew on, after about 1150, and worked up into romance: above all, into the rich many-sided romance of Arthur himself and his matchless court.

One reason why the story-tellers did it was that it brought them royal favour as well as eager audiences. Henry II came to the throne in 1154. His queen, Eleanor, had vast lands of her own in what is now western France. Their young, powerful realm needed a national glamour to equal the French glamour of Charlemagne. King Arthur supplied it. The 'Matter of Britain' was as splendid as the 'Matter of France'. As long, that is, as everybody could be persuaded to believe in it. So Henry and Eleanor encouraged the poets who were setting the fashion, and made it clear that they were graciously disposed towards anyone who helped Arthur to seem more real.

In Chapter 3 we shall discuss whether he was. The point

now is that in the later twelfth century those who knew of him at all were generally willing to think so. They took Geoffrey of Monmouth's book seriously—not only the parts that could be more or less true, but also some of the parts where Geoffrey simply must be inventing or exaggerating. Moreover, they accepted that King Henry of England, who was pulling the country together after centuries of invasions and wars, was Arthur's successor. At least, he was Arthur's successor so far as anybody was.

The only people who hotly disputed this were, of course, the Welsh. Most of them were still holding out against England. They claimed Arthur as their own property. Some had taken over the idea held by the Cornish (and probably the Bretons too) that Arthur was not dead. They foretold that he would come back in person, lead his race into victorious battle, and restore the British kingdom.

That prophecy did not suit King Henry. He replied to it by announcing that Arthur was quite definitely dead, and, furthermore, that a Welsh minstrel had given away the well-kept secret of his grave. It was in the burial ground of Glastonbury Abbey, between two pillars. Glastonbury was then surrounded by marshland and lagoons, practically an island in winter, and some claimed that it was the real Isle of Avalon.

In 1190 the monks searched for Arthur's remains, and found them. Or so they said. They dug between the pillars. Seven feet down they unearthed a stone slab, and a cross with a Latin inscription meaning 'Here lies buried the renowned King Arthur in the Isle of Avalon'. Nine feet farther down their shovels struck against an oak log. It was hollow, and inside lay the skeleton of a tall man with a damaged skull. There were also some smaller bones, with a wisp of yellow hair . . . Guinevere?

21

The Holy Grail appears to the knights at the Round Table. (14TH CENTURY FRENCH MANUSCRIPT—MANSELL COLLECTION)

Later we shall have to decide what to make of the monks' discovery. In any case it proved what the King of England wanted. Arthur would never return to help the Welsh. Henry's son Richard I, who had just succeeded to the crown, was lord of Glastonbury and rightful heir of the king who had chosen to be buried there. The bones were put in a casket, and kept in a place of honour at the Abbey. Richard improved the find by appearing with a sword which he said was Arthur's; this had also been dug up at the Abbey. But he gave away his alleged Excalibur (this was the name now preferred for Arthur's sword) to Tancred of Sicily during a crusade.

Many poets and prose authors shared in the medieval working-up of the 'Matter of Britain', from the twelfth century onward. Most of them used French, which was spoken by the better-educated in England as well as France. But presently there were tales of Arthur in English, German, Italian, and Spanish too.

The first author who mentions a Round Table is Robert Wace of Jersey. He dedicated his book to Queen Eleanor. It retells the more exciting parts of Geoffrey of Monmouth, with much romantic detail added. Wace says that when Arthur held court he seated his knights round the Table so that every place should be equal.

Another writer, with more influence, was Chrétien de Troyes. He was a kind of official poet in the service of one of Eleanor's daughters, the Countess Marie de Champagne. Chrétien may be the first to name Camelot as Arthur's chief city, though he never tells us where it was. Also he introduces two love-stories destined to become famous—the stories of Lancelot and Guinevere, and of Tristram, or Tristan, and Iseult.

With Chrétien and the authors after him, the Legend is taking on the shape that is most familiar to modern readers. Arthur is more in the background and his knights are standing out more as separate characters. Their adventures may begin at the King's court, but we lose sight of it as we follow whichever member of the Round Table is the hero for the moment, and get to know him as a person. We read about Galahad seeking the Holy Grail, or Gawain riding off to meet the enchanted Green Knight, or a tournament where the King may preside but the spotlight is on the jousters. This is not quite always true. The first great Arthurian poem in English, by Layamon, is a chronicle-epic of the King's reign and wars. But, on the other hand, the first in German is *Parzival*, by Wolfram von Eschenbach, which is mainly about the knight known in English as Percivale, and his quest for the Grail.

The 'Matter of Britain' never appealed much to the poorer folk. English peasants preferred Robin Hood and his merry men. But the aristocracy and the upper middle class went on enjoying it. There was something here for every taste—fighting and pageantry and the code of knighthood, and magic, religion, and love. The last two were especially important. 'Courtly' or romantic love between knights and ladies was made into a favourite theme by the French poets called troubadours, and it supplied one of the main interests of the Round Table stories. As for religion, it came in through the legend of the Holy Grail. The Grail was stated to be the cup or dish used by Christ at the Last Supper. Joseph of Arimathea, who took the Lord's body and laid it in his own tomb, was said to have carried the Grail to Britain and to have built the ancient church at Glastonbury. The sacred vessel had wonder-working powers. Afterwards it was lost. Several of Arthur's knights went in quest of it,

la place. Ensi q̃ fu ñt noraille del
roi artu et de mordres son fil la v il
furent tout destruit.

vant li rois ar tus voit
celui cop si dist trop do
lans. ha. diex por quoi
me laissies vos tant abaissier de
proesce terriene. et por lamor de
cestui cop veu son a dieu qu'il co
uient ichi mozir moi ou mordret.
Il tint g. glaiue gros z fort z lais
se core quanꝰ il puet del cheual

Arthur and Modred fall at Camlann. (14TH CENTURY MANUSCRIPT—
BRITISH MUSEUM)

having weird adventures, but hardly any of them were found worthy of seeing it.

To some extent the Grail stories are allegories, as *The Pilgrim's Progress*, written much later, is an allegory. But many of the Grail scenes are based on magical ideas which seem to go back to the old British religion before Christianity. Nobody knows who had kept the ideas alive, or how they got into the romances. Nevertheless they did. Medieval priests realised that there was more here than met the eye, and warned their flocks against reading about the Grail—thus, perhaps, making it a more popular theme than it would otherwise have been.

As the years went by, Arthur's admirers cared less and less whether his reign had really happened. Most of them believed in it, but in the way in which we now believe in the Wild West. We have a dim notion that once-upon-a-time the West actually was a land of cowboys and Indians, that Wyatt Earp and Billy the Kid were real people. But it doesn't make much difference to a TV western whether they were or not.

So it must have been in the Middle Ages with King Arthur and his glamorous world. In fact, there was no attempt at dark-age realism. The characters and customs were all updated. The knights wore medieval armour and knew the laws of chivalry. Still, one family in England did care whether Arthur was real or not. It did matter to the Plantagenet royal house, Henry II's descendants. They wanted a real Arthur for the sake of their own prestige as heirs of his kingdom.

Edward I was particularly concerned. During travels abroad as a young prince he met an Italian poet, Rusticiano, and lent him a volume of romances which spread the 'Matter

r dist li contes ke gñr pie
che regarda nascens les

Arthur's body lies in the boat that took him away. (14TH CENTURY MANUSCRIPT—BRITISH MUSEUM)

of Britain' in Italy. As king, Edward used to show an old crown among his regalia which he insisted was Arthur's. When he wanted to maintain that he was rightful overlord of the Scots, he quoted Geoffrey of Monmouth to prove that Arthur's kingdom of Britain had included Scotland.

His wars to subdue Wales made him very anxious indeed to keep a firm grip on belief in Arthur. For one thing, if he was Arthur's successor the Welsh should admit that they were his subjects. For another, if he could show once again that while Arthur was real he was also dead it would damp the renewed hopes of Welshmen that their hero would return to save them. So in 1278 Edward visited Glastonbury

Abbey with his queen and the Archbishop of Canterbury. The bones were taken out of the casket, put on view, and then buried in a new tomb before the high altar of the Abbey church. (The spot is marked today by a notice-board.) After years of fighting, Edward did conquer the Welsh. He asserted his title by proclaiming his son Prince of Wales—the first English heir-apparent who was so called.

Edward III was another sovereign who took King Arthur seriously. Early in his reign he made a state visit to Glastonbury. It cost the Abbot £800, a fearful amount in those days. Later Edward took a personal interest in a search for the grave of Joseph of Arimathea within the Abbey, though nothing came of this. He thought of reviving the Round Table, and did found the Order of the Garter as his own version of it.

During the thirteenth and fourteenth centuries a kind of pageant called a 'Round Table' was a standard form of courtly amusement. Round Tables were special affairs, not staged often, but spectacular when they happened. The ladies and gentlemen who took part dressed up as characters in the stories, and acted scenes from them.

In the period that began in the 1340s, a bad period for England, it looked as if Arthur's popularity might be ebbing. The Round Table hardly seemed to belong in a world where the harsh realities were the Black Death, the Peasants' Revolt, the Hundred Years' War ending in defeat, and the Wars of the Roses at home, with rival kings and their thoroughly unworthy knights cheating and murdering each other.

Foreign countries had their own troubles, and on the Continent the theme did fade out. It struck authors as old-fashioned and used up, and they gradually turned away to

Bronze statue of King Arthur in the Royal Chapel at Innsbruck, Austria.
(RADIO TIMES HULTON PICTURE LIBRARY)

other subjects. Italian poets even combined the Matters of Britain and France in a completely fanciful mixture, reviving Charlemagne but giving him a Round Table. In England, however, the 'Matter of Britain' made a comeback. The evils of the time probably helped this after all. Arthur made people think, as he had not done in better days. Under his rule (if the tale was to be believed) Britain had been great and united and successful, and chivalry had flowered. With the wars between York and Lancaster raging, the contrast was grim. Yet Englishmen could feel that they had a national ideal to cherish, the memory of a majesty which had once existed (anyhow, they had been told so) and might some day be restored.

This daydream gave a new meaning to the prophecy of Arthur's return. In spite of the Glastonbury tomb, there again began to be whispers that he was alive. And now some of the whispers were English. England had taken him over. His return would not be just an uprising of vengeful Welshmen. Not any more. It would be a revival of his glory in all Britain, with an aristocracy that behaved nobly instead of wickedly, law and order at home, and victory overseas.

If Arthur was to return in person, then he must be in some enchanted hiding-place. Perhaps Avalon was not Glastonbury, but the far-off magical isle hinted at by Geoffrey of Monmouth? The poet Lydgate favoured this view. Arthur, he declared, was 'a king y-crowned in Fairye' (Fairyland) who would reappear to reign in Britain. But there were local legends that suggested a different idea. Arthur was asleep in a cave, and would wake up when his country needed him most. Many of his knights were asleep too, in the same cave or other caves, and would join him when the hour struck. One of the most durable of these legends said that his own cave was in the Somerset hill called Cadbury Castle, and that Cadbury was the site of Camelot.

Few educated people could believe in this return of Arthur as a plain fact. Yet many could think of it as a poetic way of expressing a hope, of talking about an event that might really happen: some superb, miraculous rescue of the suffering kingdom, by Arthur's ghost, so to speak, or inspired by him. If they were unwilling to admit even that, they could still value the stories as reminding Englishmen of what kingship and knighthood ought to be—and, in Arthur's time, had been—and might yet be again.

A man who had such thoughts was Sir Thomas Malory, a knight himself; and the new version of the Legend which he composed under the influence of this kind of thinking is the one best known today. Until very recently most of the later retellings have been based on Malory, right down to T. H. White's *The Once and Future King*, which became the Broadway musical *Camelot*.

Effigy of the Black Prince in Canterbury Cathedral—one of the ambitious Plantagenets who claimed to be King Arthur's successors. (PHOTO: EDWIN SMITH)

One of the few certain things about Malory is that he spent a great deal of time locked up—perhaps as a criminal, or perhaps, more romantically, as a prisoner of war in France. Anyhow, during his spell behind bars he managed to collect a number of Arthurian books, mostly in French. These he translated into English and rewrote freely so as to make them into a linked series, giving the whole 'history' of Arthur's birth, reign, downfall, and passing. He finished the series about 1470. Caxton, the first English printer, published a shortened one-volume edition in 1485 entitled *Morte d'Arthur*, The Death of Arthur. Malory has nearly always been read in this edition. Caxton says in the preface that the book is one which many readers have urged him to bring out. Arthur's fame is still very much alive, he adds, and relics have been preserved which prove that the King and his knights were real. You can see the Round Table at Winchester and Sir Gawain's skull in Dover Castle.

We will go on now to see what happens in the Arthurian Legend according to Malory. His is so much the standard version that this is the best way to take stock of it. Still, we should bear in mind that he does not give us everything. There were different forms of all these stories before him, in several languages. Sometimes—as with the Quest of the Grail—Malory's is not the most interesting. Also there were stories of Arthur's court which he leaves out altogether, such as the tale of Sir Gawain and the Green Knight, and the one told by Chaucer's Wife of Bath.

Hence the next chapter is not a complete mini-encyclopaedia of the Legend. But it does give the main pattern, as Malory arranged it for readers after him. (A few of his spellings have been changed, for consistency.) Most of

what has been written about the Arthur of romance can be
fitted into this pattern, more or less. As for the Arthur of
history—if any—we must look for him by other methods
entirely.

Two knights glimpse the Grail in the hands of an angel. (AUBREY
BEARDSLEY ILLUSTRATION—NATIONAL LIBRARY OF SCOTLAND)

2

MALORY'S STORY

UTHER, KING OF BRITAIN, WAS
at war with the rebel Duke of Cornwall. During a truce he
met the Duke's wife Ygerne and fell in love with her. When
fighting began again the Duke sent her for safety to his castle
at Tintagel, while he withstood a siege by Uther's troops in
another place.

The prophet Merlin came to Uther and offered to serve
him. By magic Merlin made the King look like the Duke, so
that he was able to join Ygerne in Tintagel Castle. While
they were together her real husband was killed in battle.
Uther, restored to his own likeness, married her. It was some
time before he told her what had happened.

Ygerne had two sisters: Margawse, who now married
King Lot of Orkney, and Elayne, who married another local
ruler. By her previous husband, Ygerne had a daughter,
Morgan le Fay, who became a witch.

When Uther's son by Ygerne was born, Merlin took
charge of him, saying that he had a special and glorious
destiny. The wizard named the child Arthur, and gave him to
Sir Ector as a foster-son.

A few years later King Uther died, naming Arthur as his
heir. But while the prince was a boy, no one acknowledged
him as king, and Britain was torn by civil war. At last the

Archbishop of Canterbury summoned the nobles to London, promising that the rightful sovereign would be revealed. Sir Ector came with Arthur and his own son Kay. The Archbishop showed the nobles a block of marble four feet square with an anvil on top, and a sword passing down through the anvil into the stone. On the anvil was an inscription declaring that whoever could pull the sword out was the true King of Britain.

Many tried in vain. Arthur did not know of the test. But when he wanted to borrow a sword for Kay (who had left his own behind) he drew out the one in the stone with no difficulty.

Though he was now old enough to reign, his right was challenged because of the doubt that still hung round his parentage. Several local kings in the north and west rose against him. With Merlin's advice, and the magic sword in his hand, Arthur defeated them. During a campaign in the West Country he met Guinevere, the daughter of one of his allies, and loved her.

Gradually King Arthur reduced more and more of Britain to peace. When he broke his sword in combat, Merlin guided him to the Lake of Avalon, and there he saw an arm rise out of the water; the hand grasped another sword, richly jewelled, in a fine scabbard. 'That,' said Merlin, 'is Excalibur, and the Lady of the Lake will give it to you.' She came to them in a boat, and Arthur rowed over to take the sword. Merlin told him that while he wore the scabbard no wound would ever cause him to lose blood.

Arthur's wars with his many and various enemies dragged on for years. But Merlin's prophetic powers gave him an advantage, and he gained ground steadily. He held court at Camelot (which, says Malory, is the old name of Winchester) and reigned with great splendour, presiding over royal hunts and magnificent tournaments.

The wedding of Arthur and Guinevere. Oak carving in the King's Robing Room, House of Lords. (RADIO TIMES HULTON PICTURE LIBRARY)

When Arthur married Guinevere her father presented him with a Round Table which had once belonged to Uther. It could seat a hundred and fifty knights. Because of its shape, none was above or below another. Arthur took it to Camelot and appointed who should belong to his knighthood, each man's name being painted in gold on his place at the Table. One place was the *Siege Perilous*, the Perilous Seat. This was Merlin's doing. He said this place was reserved for a knight yet unborn. It would be death for anyone else to sit there.

Among the first Knights of the Round Table were Kay, Sir Ector's son; Gawain, the son of Lot of Orkney; and Pellinore, who was the senior member. Pellinore spent much of his time in pursuit of a strange monster, the Questing Beast. Many of the other knights had adventures of their own, riding out among the forests and castles of the land, to help the victims of injustice who came with their pleas to Arthur's court.

Merlin, however, was lost to Arthur. He was saddened by his foreknowledge of evil to come. The magic of the witch Morgan le Fay was already working against the King; and a boy named Modred, Arthur's cousin, or (as some whispered) secretly his son, was already marked as a threat. Merlin himself was lured from the court by another sorceress, Nyneve, who was of the household of the Lady of the Lake, and later succeeded to that title. Nyneve wanted to learn Merlin's magic arts. They wandered through Cornwall, where he showed her many enchanted places known only to magicians. At last she grew tired of him and imprisoned him in a cave by means of a spell which he had taught her himself. Later she was brought back to Camelot by Sir Pelleas, who became her lover. But Merlin never escaped.

King Arthur subdued not only the British Isles but also France. Beyond the Alps, however, it was remembered that Britain had once been tributary to Rome. The Emperor Lucius sent ambassadors to Camelot. They arrived during a feast in honour of some of the more promising knights, especially Lancelot du Lake, a nephew of Ygerne.

Lucius's ambassadors were frightened of Arthur. But they delivered their master's demand for tribute, and his threat of invasion if it should be refused. Arthur dismissed them to their lodgings and held a council to debate what answer to give. His advisers agreed that Lucius must be opposed. Arthur pointed out that according to old chronicles, several natives of Britain—Constantine, for instance—had been emperors of Rome in the past. The best defence was counter-attack: he would claim Lucius's title himself.

His chief vassals promised to supply troops, and arrangements were made for embarkation at Sandwich. Meanwhile the Roman envoys took his defiant reply to Lucius. The Emperor was angry, and summoned a vast army from the lands round the Mediterranean. Headed by fifty of the Giants of Geen, so big that no horse could carry them, the Roman host marched into France to stop the Britons.

When Arthur landed in France himself a local squire begged him to save the neighbourhood from one of the Giants of Geen, who had taken possession of Mont-Saint-Michel and was terrorising the people with banditry and cannibalism. Arthur took Sir Kay and Sir Bedevere, and they went to the fortress. Arthur found the giant chewing a man's leg, while dead children were roasting on spits turned by captive maidens. After a fearful struggle Arthur slew the giant, and thus won the support of the people for many miles round.

The Britons met a strong Roman force near Troyes and won the battle. It was here that Sir Lancelot first rose to supreme fame as a warrior. Lucius was not present himself. He advanced with his main army, but Arthur learned of his plans from a spy, and outmanoeuvred him. The battle was furious, and many of the best knights were wounded. At last Arthur broke through the Emperor's bodyguard and killed him with Excalibur.

Having restored his own authority in the places the Romans had overrun, he pushed on into Italy. Some of the fortified towns held out. But a deputation of senators and cardinals offered him the imperial crown if he would spare Rome. On Christmas Day the Pope crowned him Emperor. By now many of his knights were worried about their families and estates. So when he had found new overlords for the lands in Europe which were left in confusion by the death of their nobles, Arthur returned in triumph to Britain.

The kingdom now enjoyed a long, glorious peace, with Arthur maintaining justice, and the knights helping those in distress. Lancelot was the bravest and most courteous. But he loved Arthur's wife Guinevere, and was her own favourite among the knights.

At first their love was innocent. Lancelot's worst fault was that he grew weary of court life and rode out seeking adventures that put him in peril. On one of these he was kidnapped by the witch Morgan le Fay, on another he was assailed by giants who had seized Tintagel Castle. But he escaped from the witch and overthrew the giants and all other enemies.

No one disputed Lancelot's right to the highest honour. Second to him in prowess—according to some—was Gareth of Orkney, a brother of Gawain. Gareth served a year in disguise as a kitchen lad under Kay (who was Arthur's steward in time of peace) and finally distinguished himself in spite of many taunts. Lancelot befriended Gareth, as he befriended all good knights, without fear of rivals to himself.

Westward from Cornwall in those days, though now under the sea, lay the country of Lyonesse. Its king Melyodas married the sister of King Mark of Cornwall. She died giving birth to a son, who was named Tristram. King Melyodas married again. Tristram's stepmother jealously tried to poison him. When she was found out, Tristram pleaded with his father to spare her. Melyodas yielded, but sent Tristram away to France with a tutor.

They returned when Tristram was eighteen. He was skilled in the knightly arts of warfare, hunting, and hawking.

But also he had a polish and versatility that were rare among the knights of Britain. He could play beautifully on the harp.

Soon after his homecoming, King Angwyshaunce of Ireland demanded a tribute owed by Mark of Cornwall. Mark disavowed the debt, and insisted that the dispute should be settled by a single combat of champions. Angwyshaunce sent his wife's brother Sir Marhaus, who was a member of the Round Table and among the greatest. Mark, in consternation, appealed vainly for a knight willing to oppose him. Tristram came to his uncle's aid and defeated the challenger. A piece of his sword broke off in Marhaus's skull. Marhaus went home and died of the wound. His sister the Queen of Ireland kept the fragment of sword-blade and pondered revenge.

Tristram himself had been pierced by Marhaus's spear, and the wound did not heal, because the spear had been poisoned. He learned that the antidote could be found only in Ireland. Taking his harp, he set sail, and played so well for the Irish that he was invited to the court. Aware that he could not confess to being the slayer of Marhaus, he called himself Tramtrist. King Angwyshaunce had a daughter Iseult, who was skilled in medicine. He put Tristram in her care. She applied the antidote to the wound. While he was recovering he taught her to play the harp, and they fell ardently in love.

A Saracen knight, Palomides, also loved Iseult. Tristram vanquished him in a joust. Henceforth they were to be deadly rivals.

Tristram's disguise failed him when the Queen of Ireland found his old sword and fitted the broken piece to it. He had to go back to Britain, exchanging vows of fidelity with Iseult. For some time he lived in Cornwall with King Mark. But Mark was treacherous and vindictive. To spite Tristram

Tristram and Iseult. Chertsey Abbey tile, 12th century. (BRITISH MUSEUM)

after a quarrel, and perhaps cause his death, he sent him to the court of Ireland again to ask for Iseult as his own bride.

Tristram loyally took the message. By a happy accident he won back Angwyshaunce's goodwill. The marriage of Iseult to Mark was arranged. Tristram was to conduct her to Cornwall with her maid Brangwayne. Iseult's mother gave Brangwayne a flask of wine containing a love-potion, saying that the bride and bridegroom should drink from it at the wedding. But Tristram and Iseult drank the wine on the voyage, not knowing what it was, and so they were destined to be lovers till death.

Iseult, nevertheless, became Mark's wife as arranged. Palomides reappeared and tried to carry her off. Tristram restored her to her husband. But he had an enemy in Mark's household, Sir Andret, who caught him with Iseult and betrayed them. Mark locked her up in a leper's hut, and tried to have Tristram put to death in a chapel on the edge of a cliff. Tristram escaped by a tremendous leap, dropping down the cliff-face to the beach, where Mark's men were afraid to follow him. He made his way to the hut and rescued Iseult, and they hid together in a forest.

At last some of Mark's retainers traced them and led Iseult home. Again Tristram sustained a poisoned wound. Iseult sent a message saying that she could not cure him herself, but there was another woman doctor who could, Isolde of the Fair Hands, daughter of the King of Brittany. So Tristram went to Brittany. As it seemed to him that he had lost Iseult, he consented to a match with the Breton princess. But although they went through the marriage cere-mony, the force of his true love came back to him and they never lived together as husband and wife. A traveller from Britain reported that Sir Lancelot had spoken scornfully of his conduct, and he was grief-stricken. Meanwhile Iseult had complained to Guinevere. The Queen advised patience.

Tristram did leave his wife and return to Britain, where he distinguished himself in many exploits and rejoined Iseult, though for a while his mind was unhinged because he believed she had another lover. Palomides still crossed his path now and then. Finally, he regained his wits. Arthur admitted him to the Round Table, giving him the seat which had once belonged to Marhaus and was still vacant.

Mark, hating Tristram even more because of this honour, made new plans for his murder. Despite warnings from Lancelot, Arthur tried to reconcile them, and Tristram continued to treat Mark chivalrously and protect him against enemies. Mark, however, broke his promise of peace and persisted in scheming. Both Mark and Morgan le Fay distressed Camelot with hints about Lancelot's motives, and the intrigue, now serious, between him and Guinevere.

The poet Sir Dinadan composed a song holding Mark up to contempt. Minstrels everywhere sang it, and Mark thought Tristram was the author. Lancelot, seeing the mortal danger Tristram was in, invited him and Iseult to his own castle of Joyous Gard. There for a while they lived happily. Palomides yielded with a good grace after one last combat, became Tristram's friend, and was baptised a Christian. But the lovers could not remain at Joyous Gard for ever. In the end Tristram fell victim to a spear-thrust by Mark as he played the harp to Iseult, and the glory of the Round Table began to wane—not only because of unknightly crimes such as this but because of the scandal over the Queen; and also because of a mystery that troubled its peace, the mystery of the Holy Grail.

The Grail was the vessel used by Christ at the Last Supper. Joseph of Arimathea, in whose tomb Jesus was laid,

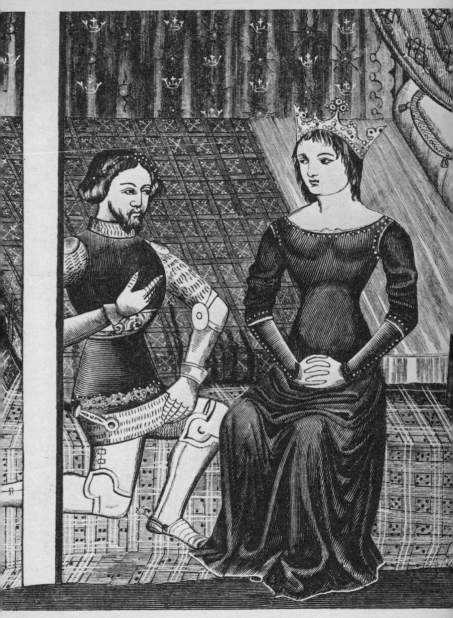

Lancelot and Guinevere. Line engraving after a French medieval miniature. (RADIO TIMES HULTON PICTURE LIBRARY)

caught some drops of his blood in it as he hung on the cross. Later Joseph carried the Grail to Britain. It had miraculous powers. By Arthur's time it had vanished. Somewhere it waited, kept by secret guardians, till a man should be born worthy to find it and restore its blessings to the land.

Sir Lancelot was strangely involved with the Grail. His love affair with the Queen, stormy and almost open, made him unworthy of the Grail himself. Yet glimpses of it had been vouchsafed to him, when he might or might not have been dreaming. And Lancelot had a son by the daughter of Pelles, a descendant of Joseph of Arimathea; that son was Galahad, who was destined to be the most saintly of the knights and achieve the Grail. When Galahad was first introduced to Camelot he sat in the *Siege Perilous* without harm, and proved in other ways that he was marked for a special fate.

It was Pentecost when Galahad came. As the knights sat at supper there was a clap of thunder and a great light, and the Holy Grail entered the hall, covered with white samite— a rich fabric of silk and gold—so that no one could see it. The apparition passed. But Gawain made a vow to go in search of the Grail, and so did many others, including Galahad. King Arthur was sorrowful. He knew the Quest would break up the Table. But he let them go. They rode out, and in spite of his sins, the gallant Lancelot was among them.

As Arthur had foreseen, many never came back. Those who sought longest and learned most were Lancelot, Gawain, Percivale, Bors, and Galahad. Their wanderings took them into unknown regions of Britain, where they saw visions and met mysterious hermits, who taught them to view their lives differently. Gawain was warned that he had stained his soul by killing men. Lancelot had to face his own guilt, yet because of his many virtues he was granted one consoling glimpse of the Grail, in the enchanted castle of Carbonek, before he returned.

Only Galahad, Percivale, and Bors were left. They, too, came to Carbonek and beheld the Grail, more constantly and distinctly than Lancelot, and with a deeper blessing. But Christ appeared and told them that it could not remain in Britain because of the sins of the people. It was to go over the sea in a ship to the Spiritual Palace in the city of Sarras.

They accompanied the Grail on its voyage. In Sarras, where Galahad was crowned king, the three of them saw the Grail for the last time. But the pure-hearted Galahad alone was permitted to gaze into it and receive its full revelation. He lived only a few more moments; the Grail was caught up to heaven, and the other knights never knew what he had seen. Percivale stayed near Sarras and died there also. Bors made his way home and told his adventures to what was left of Arthur's court. There were rejoicings, but the King knew the end was approaching. The shocks and losses of the Quest had been too heavy.

Arthur already knew, or strongly suspected, that his wife Guinevere was unfaithful. But he hated to quarrel with Lancelot, the noblest and most beloved of all his knights. Sir Modred, who hoped to stir up trouble for his own ends, encouraged Sir Aggravayne to talk of the scandal openly. Lancelot became afraid to be seen with Guinevere too often. Also he could not forget what he had glimpsed on the Grail Quest. Therefore he sometimes kept his distance from her, and she reproached him, though they always came together again.

Because of the suspicious, unknightly atmosphere that was now spreading through the court, Guinevere was accused of poisoning a guest. Lancelot was compelled to champion her in public by fighting her chief accuser. Then there was a coldness between them when Elaine, the Fair Maid of Astolat, nursed Lancelot as he lay recovering from a wound, and fell passionately in love with him. Elaine asked him directly to marry her. He replied gently that he would marry no one. She died heart-broken, asking that her body be finely dressed, placed in a boat, and rowed down the Thames. At Westminster the King and Queen saw it. A letter in Elaine's hand confirmed that Lancelot had never returned her love. Guinevere asked Lancelot to pardon her for her jealousy.

Another time, Guinevere was forcibly detained by Sir Mellyagraunce in his castle. When Lancelot rode to fetch her back Mellyagraunce's retainers shot arrows at him and hurt his horse. By Lancelot's standards the bow was a coward's weapon; times were changing. With his horse disabled, he had to ride to Mellyagraunce's castle in a borrowed cart—a disgraceful means of transport which suggested a criminal going to be hanged. After bringing the Queen home, Lancelot often used to ride in a cart as a form of bravado.

Finally, the scheming of Modred and Aggravayne succeeded. They forced Arthur to face the problem of his wife and her lover. One night when Lancelot and Guinevere were together the plotters came to the door with several other knights, and began knocking and shouting. Lancelot had a sword but no armour. He unbolted the door, and then managed to push it shut again when only one man had got in. This one he killed, and put his armour on. Then he opened the door again and killed the rest, except Modred, who escaped.

Lancelot realised sadly that the break had come. Arthur

Elaine's body is rowed down the river. (GUSTAVE DORÉ ILLUSTRATION—
MANSELL COLLECTION)

had known about this trap in advance, and now he would have no choice but to turn against Lancelot and punish the Queen. Her misconduct counted as treason, and she would be sentenced to burning at the stake. Many knights, headed by Sir Bors, took Lancelot's side. When Guinevere was about to be burnt, in Carlisle, Lancelot led his followers to the rescue and carried her off to Joyous Gard. But before he succeeded in getting her away many knights loyal to the King were killed, Sir Gareth falling unarmed and by Lancelot's own hand, though unrecognised in the confusion. After this, Gareth's brother Gawain was Lancelot's implacable enemy.

Arthur besieged Joyous Gard. The Pope urged the two great rivals to make their peace, and they were so full of grief that they might have done so. But Gawain's bitterness drove Lancelot to turn away and lead his supporters over to France, where he set up a separate kingdom. Arthur followed with an army, leaving Modred as his deputy in Britain. Months were wasted in a vain siege. Lancelot and Gawain met in single combat without either yielding. And then came news from Britain which brought Arthur home.

Modred had told the people that Arthur was dead. He had usurped the throne and taken possession of Camelot. He had asked Guinevere to marry him. She was now in the Tower of London with a few loyal nobles, and Modred was besieging her there, using guns. The Archbishop of Canterbury, savagely rebuffed in an attempt to intercede, had taken refuge at Glastonbury. This revolt was the more menacing because Modred held out alluring hopes of an end to the civil turmoil and overseas war.

Arthur's army put in at Dover. Modred failed to prevent the landing, but Gawain fell mortally wounded. Before he succumbed he wrote a letter of reconciliation to Lancelot,

Sir Bedevere casts away Excalibur. (AUBREY BEARDSLEY ILLUS-
TRATION—NATIONAL LIBRARY OF SCOTLAND)

begging him to forget all quarrels and join the King. The news that Arthur was still alive drew in many supporters. However, Modred was too powerful to defeat, at least until Lancelot should arrive with reinforcements. Arthur met Modred between the armies to discuss a truce.

Both Arthur and Modred feared treachery, and left orders with their soldiers to attack if they saw a sword unsheathed. During the parley a man was bitten by an adder. Unthinkingly he drew out his sword to kill it. At once fighting began. All the passions which Arthur's rule had kept in check now boiled over. By the end of the day both armies were destroyed and the Round Table finished for ever. Arthur personally killed Modred, but, before falling, the traitor gave him a mortal wound in the head.

Sir Bedevere, one of the few knights still unharmed, helped Arthur away through the heaps of dead and wounded, to a chapel beside a lake. The King commanded him to take Excalibur, fling it into the water, and report what happened. Bedevere could not bear to throw away the beautiful sword. He hid it and returned to the chapel, saying he had seen only the wind ruffling the water. Arthur told him to go again, but he acted as before. Now Arthur spoke angrily to him. The third time he did throw the sword away. A hand rose out of the lake and caught it, waved it three times, and drew it down.

Bedevere told what he had seen. Arthur asked to be carried to the water's edge, for the time had come when he must depart to Avalon. A boat came over the lake, with black-hooded women in it lamenting, and they bore the King away.

Alone, Bedevere walked off through the forest and came at length to Glastonbury. There he found the banished Archbishop kneeling by a new tomb. To this place, it

Arthur dying, a painting by Thomas Archer. (MANSELL COLLECTION)

seemed, the ladies had brought the body, and so in the holy ground of Glastonbury Arthur was laid to rest.

When Guinevere heard she retired to the convent at Amesbury, and lived in deep penance for all the ruin she had caused. Lancelot returned too late. He took his last leave of her and became a hermit at Glastonbury, as did six of the other surviving knights. When Guinevere died they carried the body to Glastonbury and buried the Queen beside her husband. Lancelot did not outlive her long. He was buried at Joyous Gard.

The King of Britain after Arthur was Constantine, who restored order. Of the remaining members of the Round Table, some lived out their days in religious retirement, others went to the Holy Land and perished honourably in battle against the Saracens.

There are those who say that Arthur himself did not truly die, but shall return and win fresh glory; and even on his tomb were inscribed the words *Hic iacet Arthurus, Rex quondam rexque futurus*—Here lies Arthur, king that was, king that shall be.

3

IN SEARCH OF THE FACTS

WHAT WERE THE FACTS BEhind all this?

We can put the question in more ways than one. The obvious thing to ask is: 'Was there a real King Arthur?' The answer then would be: 'Probably there was a great British leader of that name, somewhere about A.D. 500. But he wasn't much like the king in the stories, and there is no absolute proof that he lived at all.' It sounds a little disappointing. But only because we are not asking exactly the right question. In twilight regions like this it matters very much to know what questions can be usefully asked.

Suppose we say instead: 'Are the stories based on historical fact, on events that really happened, or are they pure fancy?' Then some worthwhile answers begin to come. Today, patient research is putting together a picture of Dark-Age Britain which goes far towards explaining where the Legend came from. Arthur fits into this as a believable central figure. But there is much more to it than Arthur alone.

When Geoffrey of Monmouth wrote his *History* and started the medieval craze, he told a great deal that cannot have been true. No British king ever conquered Norway, for instance. Yet some of his ideas were on the right lines. One

Dark-age people. Pictish figures on a stone, hunting and fighting.
(NATIONAL MUSEUM OF ANTIQUITIES, SCOTLAND)

way he showed this was by putting Arthur's court at Caerleon-upon-Usk. Not London, and not Winchester, the Camelot of Malory. Caerleon, the 'Legion City', was Roman. By Geoffrey's time it was no longer important. That fanciful court, placed in a Roman centre and not an English one, can guide our thoughts towards something far more solid—the Arthurian Fact, as it has been called, that underlies the Legend. To understand Arthur we must look back to the Roman Empire, of which Britain was once a part.

During the fifth century A.D. most of the western half of the Empire was overrun by hordes of barbarians. The best known were the Goths. In Britain, as we have seen, the invaders were Anglo-Saxons—that is, Angles and Saxons who were so much alike that they are often lumped together as a single people, and even spoken of in old histories as simply Saxons. They came over from the German coast and Holland in clumsy boats, as the Goths poured over the Rhine and the Alps. But events in Britain took a turn which they did not take on the Continent.

Most Gauls and Spaniards, and many Italians, no longer cared much whether the barbarians overran them or not. They sometimes took refuge, but put up little mass resistance. The Britons behaved differently. They were a Celtic nation, akin to the Irish. But whereas the Irish had never lived under Roman rule, a large number of Britons—the nobles, the rich, the educated especially—saw themselves as full citizens of the Roman Empire, standard-bearers of civilisation on the wild edge of the world.

St. Patrick was a Briton who lived at this time, and he tackled his famous mission to Ireland in that spirit. Britons like Patrick were Christians loyal to the Bishop of Rome. They used Latin as well as the Celtic British language, from which Welsh is derived. They often had Roman names:

Patrick is Patricius. They had learnt how to work the Roman system of government as Rome itself grew weaker and less able to dictate to them. After the year 410 Britain was managing her own affairs while still officially part of the Roman Empire.

When the heathen Anglo-Saxon pirates and plunderers began trying to conquer Britain they met what the Goths on the Continent never did, a genuine resistance. Here alone, the people of a Roman land had achieved independence, however shakily. They put up a fight and—for a time—won. It is in the setting of their counter-thrust against the invader that we must look for Arthur, and whatever British realm he may have controlled.

The struggle was long, with many twists and turns, and the records are so few and bad that we can only follow it roughly. This is one reason why historians speak of a dark age. The Anglo-Saxons, who had been raiding for many years on an ever-bigger scale, got their first major foothold by offering to serve a British chieftain called Vortigern. He was powerful in Britain towards the middle of the fifth century, perhaps as overlord of the whole country, and he wanted to loosen the links with the Roman world. Britain was harassed by Pictish tribes from the north. The more pro-Roman Britons asked for help from the Empire but failed to get it. Then Vortigern tried to cope with the Pictish danger by hiring Angles and Saxons as mercenary soldiers, and letting them settle in Britain with their families.

After beating the Picts, these Angles and Saxons rebelled against Vortigern themselves, and marched about Britain looting and killing. Their fellow-tribesmen poured across the North Sea to join them. But partly for the very reason that they were so terrifyingly savage—more so than the Goths on the Continent—the pro-Roman party was able to get rid

Scenes from the life of Vortigern in an old chronicle: *below*, with his
councillors; *above*, dying in a fire. (13TH CENTURY MANUSCRIPT—
BRITISH MUSEUM)

of Vortigern and organise a strong counter-attack. The first leader of this party, somewhere between 460 and 470, was Ambrosius Aurelianus. All the Britons who still thought of themselves as 'citizens' flocked to his standard. The widespread raiding grew more fitful. While some areas—Kent, East Anglia, coastal Sussex—gradually became Anglo-Saxon territory, there was a hope that Ambrosius, and the British leaders who came after him, would sooner or later bring the heathen under control.

Up to this point Geoffrey of Monmouth is not too far wrong in his main outline of fifth-century events, and he gets some of the names right. Where he goes most astray is in picturing a united Britain with a King Vortigern followed by a King Ambrosius. By now the country was breaking up into little states, each with its ruling family. The Britons only combined to fight the Angles and Saxons, and not always to do that. But even after Ambrosius's final campaigns and death, perhaps about 490, a strong leader could still pull them together. The fortune of war swayed back and forth. At last the Britons won a crushing success at the siege of Mount Badon—that cryptic battle which William of Malmesbury heard of, and Geoffrey placed at Bath.

Badon was fought after 490 and before 520. It resulted in a long spell of peace, or near-peace, with the Britons on top. For at least the first part of this time they enjoyed prosperity and good government. Although they had lost most of their Roman polish, they still clung proudly to bits of their heritage from the Empire, above all to Christianity. Meanwhile the Anglo-Saxons were halted on most fronts. Some were even leaving Britain altogether, despairing of seizing any more land for themselves. It was not till about 550 that they recovered and pushed forward again.

This unique British rally against the barbarians is the

Arthurian Fact. The tradition of a brief age of glory grew round it, and was passed on to the Britons' descendants, who kept it green long after the Anglo-Saxons turned most of Britain into England. From that tradition—Welsh, Cornish, Breton—comes all that anybody knows about Arthur as a person. The clearest statement is that he was the general (and, after all, there must have been one) who commanded the British army in its crowning victory at Mount Badon.

A very old Welsh chronicle, which notes the chief happenings in various years, has an entry against 516 or 518 (there is some doubt which year the author intends):

The battle of Badon in which Arthur carried the cross of Our Lord Jesus Christ, for three days and nights, on his shoulders, and the Britons were victorious.

Then, twenty-one years later:

The battle of Camlaun in which Arthur and Medraut were slain; and there was death in England and Ireland.

'Camlaun' is the same as Camlann, always named as the scene of Arthur's last fight, and 'Medraut' is the oldest spelling of Modred, the traitor. The dates may be wrong: one theory says twenty-odd years wrong. But we are getting facts of some sort. Perhaps the most interesting is a non-fact. The chronicle does not call Arthur a king. He is a war-leader—a Christian Briton who carries a cross emblem into battle like the crusaders.

We can read a longer account in a *History of the Britons* put together by Nennius, a Welsh monk. Nennius worked early in the ninth century, but copied from documents which are far earlier than that. Writing in Latin, he tells us that

Arthur's army meets the Saxons at Mount Badon (a medieval artist's conception). (15TH CENTURY MANUSCRIPT—BIBLIOTHÈQUE ROYALE, BRUSSELS)

Arthur was not born into the higher British nobility. However . . .

Arthur fought against the Saxons alongside the kings of the Britons, but he himself was the leader in the battles (*dux bellorum*). The first battle was at the mouth of the river which is called Glein. The next four were on the banks of another river, which is called Dubglas and is in the region Linnuis. The sixth was upon the river which is called Bassas. The seventh was in the wood of Celidon; that is, Cat Coit Celidon. The eighth was by Castle Guinnion, in which Arthur carried on his shoulders an image of St. Mary Ever-Virgin, and there was a great slaughter of them, through the strength of Our Lord Jesus

Christ and of the holy Mary his maiden-mother. The ninth was in the City of the Legion. The tenth was on the bank of the river which is called Tribruit. The eleventh was on the hill called Agned. The twelfth was on Mount Badon, in which—on that one day—there fell in one onslaught of Arthur's, nine hundred and sixty men; and none slew them but he alone, and in all his battles he remained victor.

It is plain how Nennius sees Arthur—not as one of the 'kings of the Britons' whom he aided but, again, as a war-leader. Even when the story gets exaggerated beyond belief, as it does at the end, it is that kind of exaggeration. Arthur is not said to have ruled over an absurdly great kingdom, as in the tales of the Middle Ages. He is said to have killed an absurd number of men single-handed.

The British victories are probably real enough, though Nennius may be crediting Arthur with too many of them, and adding a few which were won against other enemies, such as the Picts. The main trouble with the list is that the place-names are British, and have long since been replaced on the map by English ones. We can catch a few faint echoes. It remains very doubtful where Arthur's battlefields were.

'Glein' may be the River Glen in Lincolnshire. 'Linnuis' is likely to be the Lindsey district in the north of the same county. Arthur may well have fought a campaign against Angles entering Britain up the Wash and the Humber, as some certainly did.

'Celidon' is the same word as Caledonia, meaning what is now Scotland, and the 'forest' was probably in and around Lanark. 'Tribruit' seems to have been a river in much the same area, though nobody knows which. The 'City of the Legion' would be either Caerleon or Chester. These sites are too far from the North Sea to have been involved in the main invasion so early. However, another book speaks of a war by Arthur against British enemies in the Scottish lowlands and North Wales. Such a war could explain these three battles, and it might have drawn in all sorts of wandering warriors.

'Bassas', 'Guinnion', and 'Agned' are still mysteries, though several guesses have been tried. 'Mount Badon', of course, is the most important, and this battle is mentioned by one other historian writing close to Arthur's own time. It must have been somewhere in southern England, because a victory anywhere else could not have been so decisive—the heathen colonies in the east and north were not yet big enough to matter. One good suggestion is that the battle was fought near Swindon. Here, there is a village called Badbury overlooked by an ancient British hill-fort, Liddington Castle, its huge earthworks still well defined. Dorset has another hill-fort called Badbury Rings, but it seems a less likely place for a decisive battle. A third serious candidate is Bath.

Even through all this fog of doubt, the outline of a great British commander-in-chief does begin to loom up. The name 'Arthur' itself is worth noting. It is Artorius, a Roman name taken over by the Britons, like 'Patrick'. That alone is enough to place the man in the right kind of company— among such Britons as Ambrosius and Patrick himself, who prized what was left of the Roman heritage of civilisation and Christianity, and fought against pagan barbarism. But there is a further point about the name 'Arthur'. We have no record of any native of Britain so called before the sixth century. Then, in the later part of that century, several begin appearing, including even a prince in far-off Argyll. Almost certainly they were all named by their parents after one great

Arthur who had become a national hero. Why not in just the way Nennius implies—by saving his people in a series of brilliant campaigns?

Long before Nennius his name turns up in war-poems composed in Welsh, mostly by bards in Cumberland, which was then a British kingdom. As far back as we can trace him he is proverbial for prowess in battle. The bards never explain who he was, obviously because their audience already knows. Moreover, some of their poems name several of his followers. And the two most often mentioned are called Kei and Bedwyr. These are the men who figure in Geoffrey's *History* and the Round Table romances as Kay and Bedevere.

A long poem entitled *The Song of the Graves* lists the burial places of many British warriors, but says that Arthur's grave is a mystery—the earliest hint at a secret about his passing. In another, very puzzling poem, he goes on a voyage in search of a magic cauldron. Although the cauldron has nothing to do with Christianity, the story may be connected somehow with the Quest of the Grail.

Tales like these are, of course, unlikely to be true; they are legends that gathered round a hero. Many more, which were popular in Cornwall and Wales and northern Britain, are now lost. We know they existed because early Welsh manuscripts give summaries of them. Here we meet Arthur's wife 'Gwenhwyvaer'—Guinevere. He is said to have lived with her at a fortress in Cornwall called Kelliwic, and to have quarrelled with 'Medraut', Modred again. Other summaries mention 'Trystan', Sir Tristram. As we should expect, he is in love with 'Essyllt' or Iseult. But we are also told that he guarded a herd of pigs belonging to Mark, which Arthur tried to steal—hardly what we would expect, in that case!

Only one of these stories has survived in anything like its old shape. This is in a Welsh collection, the *Mabinogion*. Its title is *Culhwch and Olwen*. 'Culhwch' is pronounced Kilhooch, with the *ch* as in 'loch'. The tale is a wild and often comic affair, not in the least like the courtly romances of the Middle Ages. Culhwch is a gallant youth with a wicked stepmother. She lays a spell on him so that he cannot marry unless he wins Olwen, the daughter of Ysbaddaden the giant. Ysbaddaden, however, is under a spell too, and will be slain when Olwen weds. So he tries to prevent the marriage by making impossible conditions. Culhwch must clear the bushes off a hill, sow it with wheat, and harvest it, all in one day. He must find and bring back various hidden treasures. He must get a witch's blood, and he must catch a monstrous boar. For help with these and other tasks he goes to Arthur, who is his cousin, and Arthur's warriors aid him. There is a long list of them. We might call them Arthur's knights, though no Round Table is mentioned. A few have familiar names. Kei and Bedwyr are among them, and so is 'Gwalchmei', who seems to be the same as Gawain. Others are fairytale characters who can drink up seas, hear ants fifty miles off, stamp a mountain out flat, and do other unusual feats. Needless to say, all the tasks are performed.

In *Culhwch and Olwen* Arthur is hailed as a 'sovereign prince' and has a court. Yet his actual power is not clear. He has no authority over the giant. In fact, the giant claims to have some kind of authority over him. Looking in other places we find that the first titles applied to Arthur are not royal ones, but Nennius's *dux bellorum* (war-leader), and the Welsh *amherawdyr*, which comes from the Latin *imperator* meaning either 'commander-in-chief' or 'emperor'.

So who started the idea of his being a king? Was it Geoffrey of Monmouth himself? Probably not. We get some

Dark-age horseman drinking from a horn (another Pictish sculpture).
(NATIONAL MUSEUM OF ANTIQUITIES, SCOTLAND)

more clues, rather surprising clues, from yet another collection of early writings.

The sixth century was an active time in the Welsh Church. St. David lived then, and so did many other monks, scholars, and missionary preachers. Only a few, like David himself, are still counted as saints in the official sense. But the Welsh of the dark ages gave the title of 'saint' very freely, as a sort of compliment. Hence, hundreds of Lives of the Saints were written, handing on whatever was said about the holy men of Wales. Some of the Lives are so full of legends and miracles that they are nearly as far-fetched as *Culhwch and Olwen*. But there are solid facts scattered through them. And several bring Arthur in.

These Lives were written at the Abbey of Llancarfan in Glamorganshire, where the monks passed on traditions about him. The saints whom he meets are named Cadoc, Carannog, Padarn, and Gildas. Fanciful as the Lives are, they take us a step back from the fairy-tale world towards reality.

In the *Life of St. Cadoc*, Arthur appears twice, both times as a leader of warriors. Near the beginning he helps a princess to elope. She marries her lover, and Cadoc is their first son. Many years later, when Cadoc has become Abbot of Llancarfan, Arthur quarrels with him about sanctuary rights and demands cattle as recompense for a wrong which he says Cadoc has done him. The cows are duly delivered, but they change into bundles of fern. Arthur yields—understandably.

The *Life of St. Carannog* describes that saint as crossing the Bristol Channel to Dunster in Somerset. Here Arthur has a stronghold. He steals Carannog's portable altar, and only gives it back after the saint has helped him to get rid of a monster serpent that is annoying the neighbourhood.

The *Life of St. Padarn* shows Arthur trying to plunder yet another saint. Padarn, however, works a miracle. Arthur sinks in the earth up to his neck and has to apologise.

The truth behind these queer stories may be that the real Arthur seized church property to supply his army, so the monks remembered him chiefly as an unwelcome visitor making demands on them. He sounds like a local ruler who sometimes leads forces outside his home territory. Although he is powerful, both churchmen and laymen can and do stand up to him. This fits in well enough with Nennius's sketch of a war-leader fighting 'alongside the kings of the Britons'.

Arthur becomes a king himself—that is, the Latin title *rex* is given him—in two other Saints' lives. One is about Gildas, a learned, bad-tempered monk who wrote an account (though a poor one) of his country's troubles and the rescue at Mount Badon. In his *Life* Arthur is a 'rebellious king' who claims to rule over all Britain, but is opposed by other Britons, especially in the north. Melwas, the king of Somerset, kidnaps Arthur's wife and keeps her at Glastonbury. Arthur arrives with troops from Devon and Cornwall. Fearing a siege, Gildas and the Abbot arrange a treaty. The lady goes back to her husband. As we shall see, recent archaeology has shown that the story may be true. It hints that Arthur had royal power only in parts of the West Country; everywhere else his rank was open to dispute.

In one more Saint's Life, written in Brittany, Arthur is called the 'great king of the Britons' and is said to have fought on the Continent. But here we drift into the fancies of the Middle Ages. If we want facts the story does not help. It is simply an instance of the sort of thing we should now have a clearer picture of—the medley of cloudy notions about Arthur which were hovering around in the twelfth century.

These were the notions which Geoffrey and the romancers got hold of, and worked up into the Arthurian Legend, as we saw in Chapter 1.

There is not much doubt that the mass of tradition does take us back to a real person, however weird some of the tales may be. It is far easier to believe that Arthur existed than that he didn't. Certainly the Arthurian Fact—the long British rally against the invaders, the phase of triumph and peace—shows up better through the shadows of history than the leader himself. Just the same, he is there, the immortal symbol of the rally throughout its more successful stages, and (in his fellow-countrymen's eyes) the winner of all the victories. Around Arthur himself we can make out a few companions who also probably lived—Kay, Bedevere, Modred, Tristram, and Guinevere; perhaps Mark, Iseult, and Gawain. Other characters of legend, such as Merlin and Lancelot, are less likely.

Arthur was never acknowledged King of Britain, though perhaps his supporters thought he should be, and even tried to make him so. He must have started out as a minor noble or local chief. He was born somewhere about the 470s, into a Christian family that still had Roman sympathies and loyalties. As a young man he led his retainers on raiding and feuding expeditions, like some American frontiersman of a later day. He was a bolder leader than most. Followers gathered round him as a private army: we can call them his knights, so long as we don't think of them as medieval horsemen in full armour. Arthur took the field against the Anglo-Saxons, first perhaps under the command of Ambrosius. Rising to the top after Ambrosius died or retired, he helped the kings who divided Britain among them. Success made him powerful. But he was never a recognised

Liddington Castle, Wiltshire. (AEROFILMS LTD.)

overlord, except so far as he was entrusted with the supreme command in a major campaign. Also he quarrelled with the Church because he demanded its goods to sustain his war effort. That meant that no proper account of him was ever written, because the only people who wrote, the monks, had taken a dislike to him. Several times he fought his own fellow-countrymen, and he died in battle against one of them, Modred.

This is a story which fits all the facts there are. With so many gaps in it, we are free to believe, or to disbelieve, many things. A great deal more of the Legend may be true, in a way ... or it may not. How much more can we ever hope to learn for certain? At any rate, three questions are worth asking.

First, what part of Britain was Arthur's home?

Second, was he really a national commander-in-chief who went everywhere? Or did he stay near home and fight on one front? Are the hints at battles hundreds of miles apart misleading or exaggerated?

Third, how did he turn the tables on the Anglo-Saxons after so many years of doubtful warfare? Did he take them by surprise with some new weapon or tactic?

On the first question—where he came from—all traditions agree. His home was in the West Country. Even the vaguest clues point that way. From Cornwall to the Scottish Highlands there are place-names and local legends that recall him; yet there is only the one part of Britain where we find places like Tintagel where he is said to have been born, the British hill-forts in Cornwall and Somerset where he is said to have lived, and Glastonbury where he is said to have been buried.

The only argument against placing Arthur in Somerset, or Cornwall, is that the poems which first mention him were

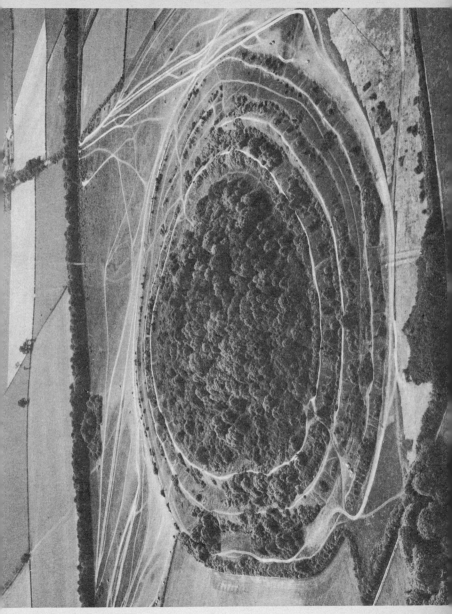

Badbury Rings, Dorset. One of these ancient hill-forts may have been the real Mount Badon. (AEROFILMS LTD.)

composed in Cumberland. His early fame seems stronger in the north than the south. But this can be explained by the answer we give to the second question. If Arthur was a wide-ranging national leader, and not just an exaggerated local one, he could have lived in the West Country where tradition says, and gone far outside to fight where Nennius says—in Lincolnshire or Scotland or anywhere else. The poets of the north sang about him, not because he lived there, but because he came there and his northern campaigns left an undying memory. It is the explanation which works best, till proof can be found one way or the other.

This brings us to the third question, and to a famous theory that tries to solve all the problems at once. It was put forward by the historian R. G. Collingwood. He pointed out that in the last years of the Roman Empire the Romans tried to turn back the barbarians with mobile cavalry forces. Early in the fifth century the defence of Britain was to have been put in the hands of a *Comes* or Count with six mounted units, as well as infantry. Britain was lost to the Empire before the Count properly organised his command. But was the arrangement revived later by the Britons themselves? Was Arthur a general who studied Roman methods of war and trained a force of heavily armoured horsemen? If so, it is easy to see how he might have won his battles. The Anglo-Saxons had no cavalry, and few of them could even ride. Easy, too, to see how he could have ranged so far, leaving a widespread fame and a tradition about an invincible band of mounted men.

Again there is no proof yet, one way or the other. Aneirin, one of the northern poets, does tell of warriors on horseback not very long after Arthur. If some future archaeologist digs up bits of cavalry equipment the figure of the Briton may become plainer to us.

74

Culhwch in Arthur's hall—as pictured by a Victorian artist. (NATIONAL
LIBRARY OF SCOTLAND)

Until then we can say this at least: that whatever Arthur was like, he left his mark on the whole history of Britain. Geoffrey of Monmouth was right in making him important, even though he got so many things wrong, and crowned him with a royalty he almost certainly never had. Arthur stopped the Anglo-Saxon advance and gave his people many years' peace. That breathing-space was what the romancers thought of as his 'reign'. In it, whatever else didn't happen, two things did.

The British Church made a stride forward, especially in Wales. Its holy men not only civilised areas of their own country which Rome had scarcely touched, they followed up St. Patrick's mission in Ireland. Through the darkest of the dark ages, western Britain and Ireland kept culture alive, safe from the barbarians. When their chance came the scholars of the Celtic West journeyed back not only to Britain but to the Continent. The darkness began to lighten when it did, largely because Arthur's victories had saved a refuge for learning in the British Isles.

There was another reason why the recovery began, and this, too, was partly his doing. Of course, the British rally failed in the end. The Anglo-Saxons did finally conquer most of Britain and turn it into 'England'. But the Anglo-Saxons who did this were no longer the bloodthirsty savages who had swarmed across the coast in the fifth century. They were descendants who had settled down, and become Christian and rather more civilised themselves. Because of the long hold-up after Mount Badon, Britain never sank into total night. The final conquest was not a slaughter but a blending of peoples, who learned, in many places, to get on with each other. Most English families today probably have Arthur's Britons among their ancestors.

So when all the critical tearing-down has been done,

Arthur remains quite impressive enough to be interesting. Having seen what we can learn from written records, let us see what we can find out about him—or at any rate, about his Britain—by another method: archaeology. Perhaps the spade can come in to help where the pen fails.

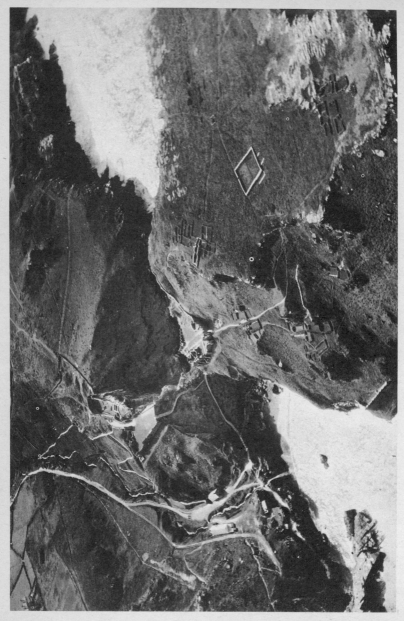

Tintagel. Aerial view of the headland and adjacent coast. The ruins near the isthmus are part of the medieval castle; many of the others are dark-age. (AEROFILMS LTD.)

4

THE CASTLE THAT WAS SOMETHING ELSE

IN MALORY THE STORY STARTS at Tintagel Castle, where Arthur is born. That idea can be traced back to Geoffrey of Monmouth. But no farther.

Is there anything in it? What can we say about this birthplace?

Certainly it is worth noting that Geoffrey locates such a momentous event in Cornwall. As he wrote chiefly for the glory of Wales, we would expect him to give a Welsh birthplace, unless there was a very strong reason not to. He must surely have heard a real Cornish tradition which was too well known to contradict. But while the case for Arthur having been born in Cornwall seems fairly good, Tintagel Castle itself is another matter. We must tread carefully.

The remains of the castle stand to this day on a high rocky headland, almost an island, overlooking the widest stretch of the Bristol Channel. But no part of the ruin is anywhere near old enough. The earliest known castle on the site was begun about 1141, when a Norman named Reginald was made Earl of Cornwall and became lord of the manor of Bossinney, which includes Tintagel. Reginald fortified the isthmus that joins the headland to the main coastline, and put up a stone hall and a chapel out on the headland itself. Afterwards other owners added much more.

However, if we go back before Reginald to Domesday Book we find nothing about a castle in the manor of Bossinney. Domesday was compiled in 1086. While early Norman fortifications can be made out in the village, there is no evidence for any such building on the headland, which is some distance off and entirely separate.

Hence Tintagel Castle can hardly be earlier than Geoffrey of Monmouth himself. Actually it is later than the first edition of his *History*. However, the text which we now have is a second edition, and it is all too likely that Geoffrey put Tintagel in when he revised the book—perhaps as a compliment to his patron Robert of Gloucester, who was related to Earl Reginald. Any vague local belief that somebody had lived on the headland before, once-upon-a-time, would have been all that Geoffrey needed to back up his yarn of another castle six hundred years previously.

If this famous scene is mainly a flight of fancy by Geoffrey, does Tintagel fade out of the picture of dark-age history, to live on only in romance?

The first great achievement of Arthurian archaeology was to prove that Tintagel survives after all. In the 1920s the Ministry of Works took over the ruined castle to preserve it as a monument. For several years C. A. Ralegh Radford, an archaeologist from Devon, excavated the site. Afterwards he wrote the guidebook which is still on sale there.

Today, more than forty years later, Dr. Radford has become a leading figure in British dark-age research which many archaeologists are carrying on. But when he tackled Tintagel he was a lonely trail-blazer. As far as other archaeologists were concerned, Arthur's Britain had never existed. They had unearthed hardly any traces of it, and they were not interested.

Patiently Ralegh Radford set to work on Tintagel, keep-

Ruins of the castle hall at Tintagel. (PHOTO: CHARLES WOOLF)

ing an open mind, not looking for anything in particular but the truth. What he uncovered was exciting and unexpected. It was not a British castle but a British monastery—a community of Christians belonging to what is called the Celtic Church: that is, the Church that flourished in the British Isles during the dark ages, out of touch with the Christianity of the Continent, before St. Augustine came to the Saxons in Kent.

The oldest objects to appear showed that the Tintagel monastery was probably founded in Arthur's lifetime. Finds of later date showed that it was lived in for centuries. There was a silver penny of King Alfred, who reigned from 871 to 899. The coin suggested that pilgrims might still have been visiting the headland even then.

We can say a little about the kind of monks who lived at Tintagel. They knew Latin, used it in their writing and services, and kept a small library of Latin books. But most of them came from the ordinary peasant stock of the West Country, and were not as well educated, on the average, as their brethren in Gaul or Italy. They probably preferred to talk in the Celtic British language, from which Welsh is derived. They wore coarse robes and had their hair cut in a special way. This haircut was the 'Celtic tonsure'. Continental monks shaved a round patch on top of the head. Celtic ones shaved a strip from ear to ear. (Some think this custom was taken over from the druids, the ancient pagan priest-magicians of the Celtic peoples.)

The monks who settled on the Tintagel headland about A.D. 500 raised an earth bank to mark the boundary. Within their bleak domain, they made the best use they could of the cramped level space among the rocks, and the scraps of pasture for animals.

They put up a block of rough stone buildings facing on to

a court, near the very brink of the cliff. Dr. Radford discovered the scanty ruins of their chapel, a shrine for holy relics, and a number of graves. It was hard to tell how each building had been used, because the structure had been altered at various times. However, he thought he could pick out a guest-house for pilgrims and visitors.

Farther towards the end of the headland were remnants of the monks' little farm, with a kiln for drying corn, and stone cattle-stalls. In another place was a building which seemed to have housed the library, with a writing-room and perhaps a school. Scattered about on the slopes were the monks' individual cells and a bathroom and dining-room. Tintagel must have housed at least forty inmates at any one time, and probably far more.

Although Dr. Radford found no traces of Arthur, his work was one of the first successful probes into Arthur's Britain—the first, in fact, on a scale big enough to have any real effect. The monastery had clearly been a major one, a centre of pilgrimage, education, and missions among the half-savage tribes. Arthur himself could scarcely have been born at Tintagel, since there was no sign of a permanent dwelling for anyone except the monks. But he might have come later as a pilgrim or guest.

Besides the buildings, Dr. Radford made a discovery which was to unlock further secrets of the dark age. Among the objects which he dug up were fragments of several kinds of pottery, destined to become famous as 'Tintagel' ware.

Two main types could be distinguished. Archaeologists now describe them as Tintagel A and B. The first was a fine red type, rather like the Samian used in Roman Britain. The pieces that were found had originally been parts of bowls. Sometimes a cross had been stamped on the bottom of the

Tintagel pottery: a reconstructed bowl. (PHOTO: CHARLES WOOLF)

bowl. Tintagel B was a paler brownish sort of pottery. In this case the pieces had come from big jars or amphorae for the storage of oil or wine.

What was so important about this pottery was that it was not British-made. Other specimens from remote places proved that it had started its career in the east Mediterranean area. It belonged to a period of somewhat over a century from about A.D. 470 onward. At that time the eastern Mediterranean—Greece, Asia Minor, Syria, Egypt, with of course the great city Constantinople—was the most civilised part of the world known to the Britons. Amphorae were employed there to store not only oil and wine but also (to judge from some specimens which have been studied in Roumania) all sorts of other things, including raisins and even nails.

So the Tintagel community was rich enough to import goods over all those hundreds of miles, in spite of the barbarians. Whether or not British monks cared about nails or raisins, they almost certainly brought in wine and oil. The pottery was a witness to far-flung trade and overseas contacts, to a Britain by no means cut off from civilisation.

But it turned out to mean more than that. Tintagel B, especially, could be dated within fairly narrow limits; it told a story; therefore if it were found in future on other sites it would be good evidence for two things. First, that the site had been an inhabited place round about Arthur's time, and could be put into the dark-age map as at least the home of somebody. Second, that any such 'somebody' must have been willing and able to use expensive imported goods—luxuries, more or less—from the Near East. If not a wealthy abbot, then very likely a chieftain or king, or, at the least, someone in contact with the household of such a person.

Tintagel ware was discovered on sites in Ireland. These could not shed much light on Arthur. But when it did begin to turn up in other places in Britain besides Tintagel, the effect was like breaking into a code message.

5

'HERE LIES DRUSTANUS'

TINTAGEL WARE PLAYED A part, though not a spectacular part, in Ralegh Radford's second discovery. He made it in the course of two seasons of digging during 1935 and 1936, at the ancient Cornish hillfort of Castle Dore, three miles from Fowey.

This district, like Tintagel, has one special legend hovering over it—the legend of Sir Tristram and the lady Iseult, wife of King Mark of Cornwall. In the earliest complete versions of the tale, written in French, we are told of Mark's hall in 'Lancien' and of his court going to worship at the church of St. Sampson. These names survive today. Near Fowey is a farm called Lantyne or Lantyan, in the parish of St. Sampson in Golant. Sampson was a British saint of the early sixth century, and the parish church is on a site where he founded an older one himself. When Ralegh Radford began work he knew that the legendary map was more or less believable as far as it went. Tristram and Mark might have been there. But had they?

He could point to one further piece of evidence—the only case where a dark-age object has been found with the name of one of Arthur's knights actually on it. A mile from Fowey in the general direction of Castle Dore stands a worn stone pillar seven feet tall. It was set up on its present base after

Castle Dore. The hill-fort where King Mark, Tristram's uncle, may have lived. (PHOTO: J. K. ST. JOSEPH—CAMBRIDGE UNIVERSITY COLLECTION)

being found lying flat, two hundred yards away. Down one face of it, in sixth-century lettering, are the words

DRUSTANUS HIC IACIT
FILIUS CUNOMORI

'Here lies Drustanus the son of Cunomorus.' Now 'Drustanus' is a form of the name which the medieval romancers made into 'Tristan' and then 'Tristram'. As for 'Cunomorus', it is a Latin form of Cynvawr, and a royal family tree does list a sixth-century West Country ruler named Cynvawr.

The man buried under the stone could have been the original Sir Tristram. The question facing Ralegh Radford was whether he could fill out the picture by finding the hall which King Mark was supposed to have had in that neighbourhood.

Castle Dore, where he dug, is in the right parish—St. Sampson in Golant. It is a British earthwork citadel on top of a hill, dating from long before Arthur's day. Two bank-and-ditch defences surround an inner enclosure 220 feet across. After the Roman conquest it was deserted. But Dr. Radford discovered that this was not the end of its story. About the fifth or sixth century A.D. somebody had moved back on to the hill-top. A cobbled road had been made, leading in through the gateway to a lookout platform. There had been, possibly, an attempt to improve a small stretch of the derelict rampart.

No ruins emerged—but something else did. Dr. Radford knew that even when a building has vanished, an archaeologist can often make out where it was, because it leaves a sort of ghost behind. With a wooden building, that ghost may take the form of a pattern of post-holes. Post-holes are small pits sunk into the bedrock to hold the timber posts of a structure. When a post was safely in its hole, sticking up

Tristram with Mark. Chertsey Abbey tile, 12th century. (BRITISH MUSEUM)

vertically, the builders would pack it round with rubble or other material to hold it firm. Hundreds or thousands of years later the walls that were secured to the posts may have gone, the posts themselves may have rotted away, yet the holes down below will still be there, filled with stuff of a different colour and texture from the surrounding rock. As an archaeologist once remarked, 'There are few things more difficult to destroy than a hole.'

Removing the turf and topsoil over a wide area inside the earthworks, Dr. Radford looked first for a floor. He drew blank. Generations of ploughing had blotted out whatever there might have been. But below that level he searched for the tell-tale splotches which would show where the pillars of a hall might have been sunk into the rock. These he did find: not just one post-hole but many, and not a mere sprinkling but a regular plan in several rows. He could make out where upright timbers had once been planted to support walls, and where others, inside, had risen to hold a roof up. Most of the uprights had evidently been thick, some over a foot across, implying a fairly solid building—though the rows were none too straight, and it looked as if the timbers had not been very evenly shaped. Here, then, was the ghost of the hall he was looking for. It had been ninety feet long, forty feet wide.

There were similar traces of other wooden buildings, barns perhaps. And the date was fixed by some more Tintagel pottery—very little, but just enough. This imposing hall in the old hill-fort had been the home of a British chief of about Arthur's time.

Mark himself? Nobody can tell for sure. An archaeologist is very lucky indeed if his excavations prove the existence of any particular person. Still, here at least was an impressive building of the Arthurian age (or its shadow) in exactly the right place to fit in with the story of Tristram and Iseult.

Tristram's monument. The stone near Fowey which has an early form of his name inscribed on it. (PHOTO: CHARLES WOOLF)

6

THE KINGS OF THE BRITONS AT HOME

BY HIS CORNISH WORK
Ralegh Radford achieved two important results. He found
the key clue of Tintagel pottery, and he showed that at least
one dark-age British chief reoccupied an ancient hill-fort
after it had stood deserted for over four hundred years.

Dr. Radford's discoveries were not widely known till after
the Second World War. In the 1950s, however, results of the
same kind began to emerge from a number of digs in Wales.

One hill-fort which had been pointed out by tradition for
centuries was Dinas Emrys, near Snowdon. 'Emrys' is the
Welsh form of the Roman name Ambrosius. The small
earthwork citadel was said to have belonged to Ambrosius
Aurelianus, who led the British war-effort against the Saxons
in the later fifth century, before Arthur took over. Dr. H. N.
Savory, of the National Museum of Wales, examined the site
and proved that somebody had indeed occupied it at about
the right time—a 'somebody' who seemed to have been
fairly well off, to judge from his possessions, and to have had
a smithy and a jewellery workshop.

At Degannwy, by the River Conway, is another hill which
has also been named for a long time as the home of a dark-
age ruler—Maelgwn, the king of Gwynedd or North-West
Wales, who reigned in the later part of Arthur's life and died

Dinas Powys. Leslie Alcock's diggers unearthing the foundations of a dark-age hall. (PHOTO: LESLIE ALCOCK)

about 547. Maelgwn looms large in history and legend. He was called 'the Dragon of the Isle', and claimed highest rank among the kings of the Britons. A story tells how the famous bard Taliesin made his first public appearance at Maelgwn's court as a boy.

Degannwy was excavated during the early 1960s by Leslie Alcock, of University College, Cardiff. On the higher of its two hills, under the remains of a medieval castle, he found the tell-tale Tintagel-B ware. This and other relics of the sixth century made it clear that Maelgwn had indeed lived where tradition said. In this case the Romans had used the hill previously, perhaps as a strong point against Irish raiders. There is some reason to think that the officer in charge may have handed it over by treaty to one of Maelgwn's ancestors.

Meanwhile other digs were revealing that several more Welsh hills had been occupied in the same way. Some were ancient forts, some were not. They could not be connected with well-known figures like Ambrosius and Maelgwn, but they told much the same story. Most interesting of all was Dinas Powys near Cardiff, also excavated by Mr. Alcock. Here, as at Degannwy, a medieval castle had stood on the hill. But its tumbled walls were mingled with the remains of a far older rampart and ditch. During the fifth and sixth centuries a British chieftain had lived on the site. He built a hall forty or fifty feet long, with very thick unmortared stone walls, and a hearth at one end (where no doubt he sat with his family on winter nights, while his henchmen shivered at the other). Beside the hall was a barn or storehouse, and round about the foundations were many traces of iron-smelting and other kinds of metal-working, including the manufacture of brooches. Combs, cooking dishes, and other vessels and utensils added vividly to the picture.

Here and there in Wales, there are dark-age memorial stones like Tristram's in Cornwall. With the aid of the inscriptions on these, it has become possible to say more and more about the kind of men the Arthurian citadel-owners were. They were not mere barbarians. The Latin language survived, and some of the nobles as well as the clergy were well-read. The little Welsh courts gave employment to fine craftsmen and minstrels. Wales had professional doctors, and men who still called themselves 'citizens' in the Roman sense.

The chieftains, moreover, seem to have lived quite peaceably at home, however much they made war outside. If they made use of an old hill-fort they used it in a different way from the original Iron Age builders. The ancient forts were planned as places of safety for entire tribes, and they are often large, covering acres of ground. But when dark-age occupants moved in they did not settle hordes of people inside. The dwellings of 'Emrys' and those like him are simply homesteads for one prominent household. The remains are dwarfed by the earthworks round.

While the lord of a hill did sometimes put up a wall of his own, it was usually a half-hearted affair. Certainly there is no known instance in Wales of a dark-age occupant of an ancient hill-fort seriously rebuilding or reinforcing the ramparts which he found there. The hills were not the strongholds of swarms of warriors. When they were lived in, these homesteads must have looked quiet and even rustic, far less forbidding than the huge castles imagined by Malory.

7

THE TOMB AND
THE TOR

GLASTONBURY IS THE PLACE
where the legends of King Arthur cluster most thickly. In
the ruined Abbey you can still see the notice-board marking
the spot where the hero's bones lay during the Middle Ages.
Near by is the strange hill called the Tor, with a tower on the
summit. Centuries ago, before the Somerset marshes were
drained, the Tor overlooked sheets of water, and the belief
that Glastonbury is the true Isle of Avalon has certainly
been held for a very long time.

According to the best-known version of the Grail story,
this was where Joseph of Arimathea came. The small wattle-
work church which he was said to have built was un-
doubtedly standing in Saxon and Norman times, on the site
now filled by the Lady Chapel, and was so old that nobody
knew how it had got there. Tradition further told of a community of British monks, visited by St. David and others.

Arthur himself is said to have come to Glastonbury at
least twice. The first time was when Melwas, the king of
Somerset, carried off Guinevere and kept her in his
Glastonbury stronghold, and Arthur arrived with soldiers to
recover her. This is the earliest known form of a tale which
turns up in the romances in several versions. Later Lancelot
becomes the rescuer, and Guinevere's kidnapper Melwas
becomes 'Meleagant' or, as in Malory, 'Mellyagraunce'.

Glastonbury Tor, with the tower of St. Michael's chapel on top.
(PHOTO: PITKIN PICTORIALS LTD.)

The other time Arthur came to Glastonbury was to die ... that is, if he ever did die. In 1190, as we saw, the monks dug up his grave, which was near the south wall of the Lady Chapel. Their account of their find—the space between two pillars, the stone and the leaden cross seven feet down, the hollowed log nine feet farther down, the skeleton inside it—was a strange one and has often been written off as a pure invention, a money-raising publicity stunt. But was it?

Glastonbury Abbey was Ralegh Radford's third Arthurian site. He worked there during the 1950s and early 1960s, finding the Saxon monastery and the British one before that, with wattle buildings as described. At least the monastery did seem to have been there in Arthur's day, and its cemetery had been in the right place.

When he came to the spot where Arthur's grave was supposed to have been, he knew it was too much to hope that the story could be proved completely, because the monks had put Arthur's bones in another sepulchre and they were afterwards lost. But there was no doubt that the 'pillars' had been there, just as stated. They were on top of stone shrines, and Dr. Radford unearthed some traces of them. In 1962 he also established that the earth between them had once been dug out to a great depth, that the hole had been filled up again, and that the soil which was put in contained chips of building stone which could be dated to about 1190. At the bottom of the hole was the rough stone lining of a very early grave.

So the monks had told the truth—as far as Dr. Radford could check them. They had dug down between two pillars, and they had struck an ancient grave. What about the stone and the inscribed lead cross discovered on the way down? The cross, long treasured at the Abbey, was lost in the eighteenth century, but accurate drawings of it survive. Dr. Radford had already studied the style of lettering and judged

Aerial view of Glastonbury, showing the Abbey ruins and the Tor beyond. (AEROFILMS LTD.)

Part of the ruined church of Glastonbury Abbey. (MANSELL COLLEC-
TION)

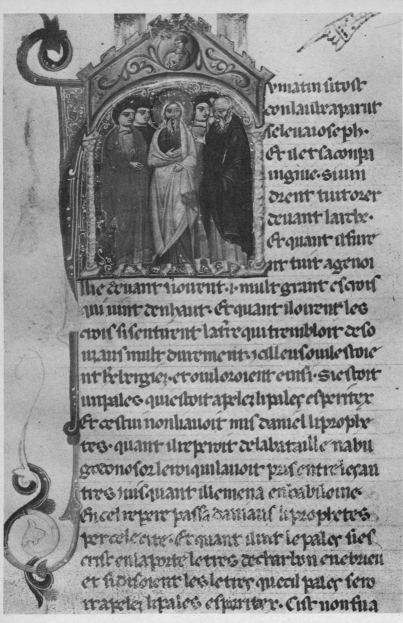

Joseph of Arimathea. An illustration in a medieval romance. (14TH CENTURY MANUSCRIPT—BODLEIAN LIBRARY, OXFORD)

Hawthorne ſic vocamus) quæ ipſo Chriſti natali, perinde ac menſe Maio, progerminat;
Hæc tamen veriſſima (ſi qua fides) plurimi fide digni produnt. Antequam me hinc re-
cipiam, accipe paucis, quod pluribus Giraldus Cambrenſis oculatus teſtis, de ſepulchro
Arthuri in huius cœmiterio retulit.

Cum Henricus Secundus Rex Angliæ ex Bardorum Britannicorum cantilenis acce-
piſſet Arthurum Britannorum nobiliſſimum heroem, qui Saxonum furores virtute ſæpe

**Arthurus
bellicoſus.**
fregerat, Glaſconiæ inter duas Pyramides ſitum eſſe, corpus inueſtigari curauit : vixque
iam ſeptem pedes in terram defodiſſent, cùm inciderent in cippum, ſiue lapidem , cuius
aduerſæ parti rudis crux plumbea, latiori forma, inſerta : quæ extracta inſcriptas literas
oſtendit, & ſub eo ad nouen ferè pedum altitudinem, ſepulchrum inuentum , ex quercu
cauata, in qua oſſa inclyti illius Arthuri repoſita. Inſcriptionem autem ex Prototypo , in
Glaſconienſi cœnobio quondam deſcriptam, propter literarum antiquitatem ſubiungen-
dam putaui. Barbarum quiddam, & quaſi Gothicum præ ſe ferunt literæ, & eius ætatis
barbariem planè loquuntur, quæ adeo fatalibus tenebris inuoluta erat , vt nemo fuerit,
cuius ſcriptis Arthuri nomen celebraretur. Materies proculdubiò doctiſſimi viri faculta-
te, & copia digna , qui tantum principem celebrando propriam etiam ingenij laudem
conſecutus fuiſſet. Fortiſſimus enim Britannici imperij propugnator hoc ſolo nomine
vel infœliciſſimus videtur, quòd ſuæ virtutis dignum præconem non inuenerit. Sed ecce
crucem illam & inſcriptionem :

Nec

Page from Camden's book *Britannia*, published in 1607, with drawing
of the cross found in Arthur's grave. (JOHN R. FREEMAN & CO. LTD.)

that it had not been faked in the twelfth century. On the other hand, it could hardly be as early as Arthur. It looked like Saxon lettering, probably of the tenth century when the great St. Dunstan was Abbot of Glastonbury.

Could the facts be fitted together? There was one fact more, and it made sense of the whole puzzle. In the Life of St. Dunstan it is recorded that he remodelled the cemetery. So many monks had been buried that there was no room for any more graves. His solution was to pile up a thick new layer of earth on top.

Dr. Radford suggested that what had happened was this. Arthur was buried in an honourable place near the shrines of the saints. On the surface nine feet above his coffin a memorial monolith was set up like Tristram's. In the tenth century Dunstan's monks inscribed the cross and placed it beside the stone as an additional marker. But afterwards they piled their fresh layer of earth on top, and the stone and the cross were buried together to a depth of seven feet. Hence in 1190, when the monks of that day started digging from the raised ground-level in search of Arthur, they went down through Dunstan's layer to the stone and the cross, and then on down through the level of the old cemetery to Arthur's coffin.

It was too much to believe that the monks of 1190 could have made up such a strange, complicated, yet plausible tale. They must have actually done what they said, and found the bones of a man who had been identified as Arthur much earlier. There could be no final proof that he actually was. But there was no reason to think that he was anyone else.

The other story of Arthur at Glastonbury was also partly borne out in 1964–6, when Philip Rahtz of Birmingham University excavated the summit of the Tor. He found plentiful remains of a small dark-age stronghold, where someone had lived in much the same style as the Welsh chieftains. The citadel of Melwas? Why not?

8

IS IT CAMELOT?

bury Tor looked south-eastward over the Vale of Avalon he saw a line of hills on the horizon. One of them—perhaps—was the home of the lady he carried off. And from somewhere near it—perhaps—her husband was later brought, dying or dead, to his burial in the monks' graveyard.

Cadbury Castle has always been the likeliest site of the 'real Camelot'—that is, the HQ of the real Arthur. But it was only in 1966 that its full story began to unfold.

The hill is about five hundred feet high. It stands apart from the neighbouring hills, which form the edge of the Dorset uplands. There has never been a castle here in the Norman or Plantagenet sense. Cadbury is another ancient British hill-fort, with four lines of immense earthwork ramparts, defending an eighteen-acre enclosure on top. Today the earthworks are largely overgrown with trees. The main path from South Cadbury village leads steeply up to a break in the topmost bank. The old entrance, however, is on the other, south-western side. Within easy walking distance are the village of Queen Camel, originally plain Camel, and a river Cam. It has been claimed that the river is the scene of Arthur's last battle, Camlann, and skeletons are said to have been dug up in a field, as if many men had been buried at the same time.

105

Cadbury Castle from the air. (PHOTO: H. J. P. ARNOLD)

John Leland, one of the chief historians in the reign of Henry VIII, visited the neighbourhood and wrote:

> At South Cadbyri standith Camallate, sumtyme a famose toun or castelle. The people can tell nothing thar but that they have hard say that Arture much resortid to Camalat.

Leland does not discuss this as if it were a problem. He simply takes it for granted that the hill-fort is properly so called, and passes on. Many others seem to have thought the same. There are local legends, certainly very ancient, which tell of the cave somewhere in the hill where Arthur lies asleep and will one day wake. The plateau on top is 'King Arthur's Palace'. On St. John's Eve at midsummer it is said that you can hear the ghostly hoof-beats of the King's horse and those of his knights as they ride down through the south-west gate for the horses to be watered at a spring.

From the nineteenth century onward archaeologists were looking at the hill wondering what secrets it harboured. One of them even dug in 1913, on a small scale, finding traces of inhabitants before the Roman conquest. But Cadbury was simply too huge. Where could a proper excavation start? Who would finance it? Was there likely to be anything in the Camelot story, anyhow?

Signs that there might be came at last in the 1950s. The clue was the same as in other places—Tintagel pottery. The soil on the top is very shallow, because it has often been disturbed by ploughing and heavy rain, and keeps getting washed downhill. Mrs. M. Harfield, a keen amateur archaeologist, used to stroll over the summit with her dog and an umbrella, literally poking about in the jumbled top-soil. She turned up many small bits of pottery of different periods. Most of it dated from before the Romans. But a few pieces were dark-age imported ware.

Trench cut through the Cadbury earthworks, 1967. (PHOTO: LESLIE ALCOCK)

This meant that the Camelot tradition could at least be taken seriously. More and more people now urged that excavation ought to be tried. Finally, a Camelot Research Committee was formed. Ralegh Radford was Chairman; Sir Mortimer Wheeler, one of the most famous archaeologists in England, agreed to be President; and the excavations were directed by Leslie Alcock, who had been in charge at Maelgwn's Degannwy citadel and at Dinas Powys.

He began with a cautious reconnaissance in July and August 1966. The first problem was to decide where to look, in such a vast enclosure. Guided partly by hints from aerial photography, he opened up three trial sites at widely separated places. One was on the summit plateau, one was half-way down towards the top rampart, one was close beside the rampart itself and was afterwards extended to cut right through it.

Very soon it was plain that Cadbury Castle had been lived in, on and off, for thousands of years. Occupation before the Romans stretched away backwards into a dim past. The Romans had evidently captured the hill and moved the Britons out, but there were traces of a temple built towards the end of the fourth century A.D. More dark-age material confirmed the 'Arthurian' phase. Lastly, it was discovered that a stone wall had been built on top of the earthworks in the reign of Ethelred the Unready, about 1010–20, to mark the boundary of a Saxon settlement where coins were minted. Post-holes came to light on the summit—big ones, which meant a big building—though they could not be dated.

From the Camelot point of view, the most encouraging fact was that dark-age material was unearthed in all three of the trial pits. As these accounted for only one-seven-hundredth of the whole area, and were far apart from each other, it looked as if the dark-age settlement must have covered plenty of ground. Otherwise the odds against three lucky hits out of three would have been far too long.

Aided by these proofs, the Camelot Research Committee raised a large sum of money, and dug the following year on a much bigger scale. Hundreds of volunteers came forward, some from overseas. New scientific instruments, including a radar-type device nicknamed 'the banjo', were used to map out the contours of the invisible bedrock under the topsoil, and pick out places where there might be the foundations of buildings.

The 1967 dig—which was filmed for television, and watched by five thousand visitors—confirmed the picture which the first study had suggested. Cadbury Castle, like Troy, was lived in by a whole series of people. There were Neolithic inhabitants about 3000 B.C. There was a major Iron Age settlement that flourished till the Roman conquest, after A.D. 43. There was the dark-age occupation, which could be Arthur's. There was the period in the eleventh century when Cadbury Castle was the site of a Saxon mint. Also there were strange, unexplained finds, such as what seemed to be the foundation of a cross-shaped church which was never actually built.

But the excavation revealed one thing that was startling and entirely novel. The topmost earthwork rampart had been rebuilt several times. The Iron Age Britons had strengthened it with a series of new stone walls, which came to light one on top of another, with centuries of time sandwiched between. A thick layer of soil showed how the barrier had fallen into neglect and decay during the Roman age, and got silted up. But on top of this again were the tumbled remnants of a huge stone rampart twenty feet thick, with holes in it marking the bases of a vanished stockade and wooden watch-

Some of the first 'Arthurian' finds at Cadbury. The pottery fragments are Tintagel ware; the button is early Saxon, perhaps from a prisoner; one of the corroded knives probably dates from Arthur's time. (PHOTO: LESLIE ALCOCK)

towers. This rampart must have been built in or about the sixth century. In other words, it was built by Arthur ... or whoever was lord of Cadbury at that time. He had done what none of the Welsh chieftains did: reoccupied an ancient hill-citadel on a large scale, and refortified it on a very large scale indeed.

Cadbury Castle had belonged, at the right time, to somebody who at least fitted the picture of the real Arthur—a great military leader of unique status, in possession of a stronghold vastly bigger than any of the Welsh strongholds (or Glastonbury or Castle Dore), and defending it with a colossal ring of fortifications well over half a mile long. At the very least, Mr. Alcock said, an Arthur-type figure!

In 1968 the team delved into the hill a third time. They explored the south-west gate, finding more traces of the dark-age inhabitants, as well as Saxons and others. All of these had worked on the gate, modelling and remodelling, laying down a cobbled road surface, and probably putting up an arch of some kind. The same season of work located the first foundation of an Arthurian building, a hall, in a commanding central position—close to that topmost piece of ground which had always been known locally as King Arthur's Palace.

Work went on till 1970. Nothing was found with Arthur's name on it, and the diggers had always known that they would be fantastically lucky if they ever did. But they confirmed that the traditional Camelot was the home, at the right time, of a mighty British leader of the right sort. No dark-age citadel like Cadbury has been found anywhere else in Britain. It certainly seems to have been the fortress of someone unique—and if not Arthur, who?

9

WHAT ARTHUR'S BRITAIN WAS REALLY LIKE

ALTHOUGH SOME OF THE digging has had such exciting results, neither this nor any other kind of research will give us a clear notion of the way people lived, unless we can picture the simple, ordinary things.

For instance, how did the Britons dress? If you think about this question you will see the difficulty of answering it. An archaeologist may be lucky enough to find solid items like jewellery. But in a damp climate, garments like shirts and stockings will rot away.

Outside Britain the rotting-away has not always been complete. Denmark, Germany, and Holland have peat bogs which preserve objects below the surface. Among them, dark-age clothes have been found. Most of the Britons probably wore much the same. There was a slight hangover of Roman fashions among the nobles. But we can piece together a fairly detailed image by studying remains like those in the bogs, plus jewellery, ornaments, and other hard items which have not decayed. Also we must use every hint from early authors who give us glimpses of British customs.

First, then, the everyday outfit of a man. He would usually have worn a tunic. This was a sort of heavy woollen shirt, pulled on over the head, and reaching the knees. The

Sixth-century sword hilt found in Kent. (CITY OF LIVERPOOL MUSEUM)

neck was round. The sleeves might be of any length. A leather belt gathered the tunic in at the waist. In cold weather the wearer could put on several tunics at once. The wealthier Britons may also have worn light undershirts of imported linen.

The lower garment was a loose pair of trousers made of wool cloth or skins. It was held up by a rawhide thong at the waist, threaded through holes or loops. More thongs drawn tight round the ankles prevented the ends from flapping, and were sometimes wound higher up the leg to make puttees or cross-gartering.

Out of doors, as a form of overcoat, the man would wear a plain cloak. In effect, this was a woollen blanket, though it might be fur-lined, or made of skins. It was fastened on the chest or right shoulder with a large brooch—what the Romans called a *fibula*.

Shoes were rough and simple, rather like moccasins. Roman-type sandals were also made.

A woman's main dress was a tunic like the man's but ankle-length or nearly so. Her belt would be more decorative, and she might attach a purse to it. Over the tunic she could wear a gown reaching to the knee, or a cloak, or both. The undergarment was a lighter and briefer tunic—of linen, for those who could afford it.

Both men and women grew their hair longer than the Romans. Most men had beards. However, Britons used razors, combs, and scissors for trimming and tidying, with the aid of metal hand-mirrors. Soft caps of wool or fur were sometimes worn on the head, and women of high rank had light gold bands round their foreheads.

A British crowd would have been colourful. Not all clothes were plain in their pattern. Stripes and checks were probably common—perhaps, even, some early versions of

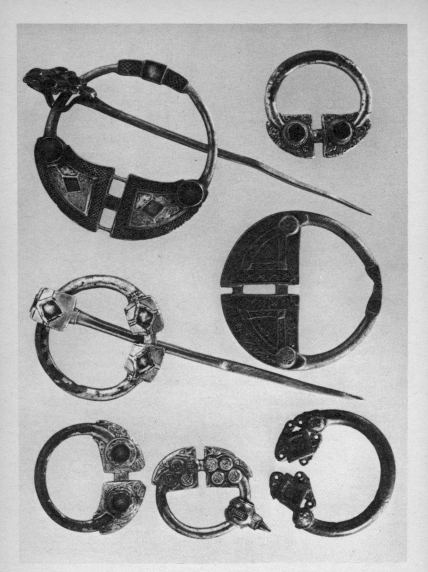

Celtic brooches. These are Irish, but the Britons made similar ones. (BRITISH MUSEUM)

the plaid. Bright vegetable dyes had been known in Britain for centuries: red from the madder root, yellow from saffron flowers, blue from woad, green from the plant now called dyer's greenweed.

The fifth century brought a rich revival of the old Celtic art which Roman fashions had blotted out. Its special feature was a complex use of abstract designs in linear tracery. Ornaments of gold, bronze, and iron were decorated in this way, and with patterned stones and enamel. The nobles wore golden collars, necklaces, diadems.

Arthur himself and his officers probably dressed in much the same style as other men, but added various extras when they went to war. Over the tunic the original Bedevere or Kay would have put on an outer tunic of tough leather, covering the body and thighs. On top of this was a coat of mail made of metal rings, something like the chain-mail of the Middle Ages, but not so small or close. Leather breeches might be worn over (or instead of) the usual trousers, with a higher type of boot than civilians had.

Helmets in this period were crude. Foot-soldiers seldom had them. Horsemen wore metal caps made of several pieces of metal riveted together, with flaps guarding the neck and ears. In Britain the metal pieces may have been fixed to a basic cap of leather.

A British warrior's sword was the long-bladed kind known as a *spatha*, not the short sword of the Roman legionary in Caesar's day. His shield was round and whitewashed. He might have an emblem painted on it—a cross, or a dragon, the symbol of power in Arthur's Britain. Other weapons were spears with diamond-shaped iron heads, javelins, daggers, and possibly slings and light battle-axes. It is curious that the oldest Welsh poetry, describing wars fought in the north soon after Arthur, never mentions bows or arrows.

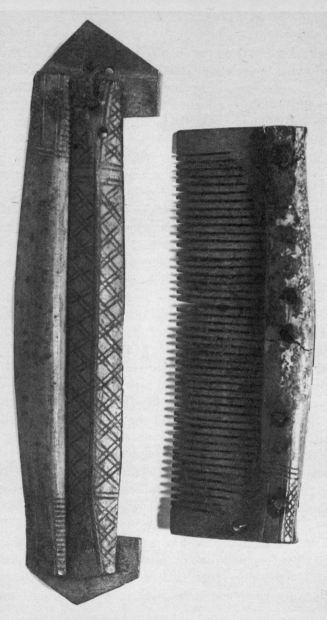

Dark-age comb (an Anglo-Saxon specimen). (BRITISH MUSEUM)

The bards who composed this poetry tell us a little of dark-age British customs in other matters besides dress. Bards were important people. Each of the kings who divided most of Britain among them kept at least one attached to his court. The bard sang songs and told tales in the royal hall. But he was far more than a minstrel. He was an all-round wise man who knew all the things it was necessary to know.

Who, for instance, were the king's father and grandfather and great-grandfather? His right to reign depended on his family tree, and the bard had this off by heart. What were the customs of the various districts in the kingdom? Which families had special honours, or owed the king special services? And always, why? Could a landowner claim freedom from taxes because his great-great-uncle had been mayor of Silchester under the Romans? Could a tribe be called upon for forced labour because they had run away during a Saxon raid? These were the sort of questions that the bard might be asked to settle, out of his knowledge of the traditions of the people.

Hence in Arthur's Britain, and in parts of it such as Wales that stayed independent for a long time, the court poets influenced the making of laws. The oldest Welsh code of laws dates from centuries after Arthur. But sections of it are copied from law-books much closer to him, and these show the bards' influence. The laws are well written, interesting, and full of vivid sidelights on British life. Here is one that lays down the fine to be paid for killing or stealing the cat who guards a royal barn:

Its head is to be held downwards on a clean, level floor, and its tail is to be held upwards; and after that, wheat must be poured over it until the tip of its tail is hidden, and that is its value.

A lady and her maid. The drawing is medieval, but may not be far wrong for the time of Arthur. (BRITISH MUSEUM MANUSCRIPT)

This law has had a note added to it by someone who was clearly a cat fancier. He tells what he looks for when judging one:

> It should be perfect of ear, perfect of eye, perfect of teeth, perfect of claw, without marks of fire, and it should kill mice, and not devour its kittens, and should not go caterwauling every new moon.

The laws, poems, and so on help us to grasp how the little kingdoms worked, and what kind of authorities Arthur had to deal with when he organised his campaigns. A king ruled by right as the previous king's heir. However, he was not always the previous king's eldest son, or his son at all. The title could go through other male relatives or the mother. Several royal families traced their claim to Rome. An ancestor who had held some Roman office—as a local governor, say—was supposed to have succeeded to part of Rome's authority when Britain drifted off into independence. Some British kings even said they were descended from emperors. Most of these claims were far-fetched. But there was probably some truth in the royal pedigrees that named the Emperor Maximus, a pretender who was proclaimed in Britain in the year 383. Maximus seems to have had a British wife, and he became a hero of legend in Wales and Cornwall—there is a romantic tale about him in the *Mabinogion*, the same collection that has *Culhwch and Olwen* in it. To this day, some Welshmen trace their family trees all the way back to 'Macsen', as he is called.

The leading British kings of the sixth century ruled over Strathclyde in the Scottish Lowlands (Dumbarton means 'fort of the Britons'); Rheged in and around Cumberland; Elmet in Yorkshire; Gwynedd in North Wales, Powys in central Wales, Dyfed in south-west Wales; the Bath–Gloucester–Cirencester area; and Dumnonia, stretching from Somerset to Land's End.

Each king had his band of nobles. They expected him to uphold their local rights, and they kept him in his state and rallied round him in war. His power depended not only on his family ties but on his own qualities, especially prowess as a fighter. This was tragic, because the kings were tempted to build themselves up by making war on each other.

The nobles spent much of the time close to their king. Poets describe their feasts in the royal halls. To judge from archaeology so far, the halls were not as splendid as the poets pretend. The one at Dinas Powys is only forty feet long. Out of doors, the nobles' main sport was hunting. They roamed the hills with their big dogs (Britain was always famous for hunting-dogs) chasing wild boar, and deer, and grouse. Or they rowed out to fish in coracles made of hides stretched over a frame.

Below this level, Britain had three ranks of people—free tribesmen and citizens, serfs who did most of the heavy field work, and slave labourers who belonged to the richer households. The free included not only the landowners but also many artists and skilled craftsmen. We have already had a glimpse of them at Dinas Powys. They were held in honour, and often travelled among the richer households selling their services.

They did not normally work for cash payments. So far as we know, Britain was not minting any coins at all, though a few may have been in circulation from abroad. Trading was by barter. Rents and taxes were paid in goods. The country's main wealth was in its farms and livestock. On the dark-age sites that have been explored animal bones are turned up by the hundred, and nearly all are from farm animals—cattle and pigs and sheep. From these came meat and milk, cheese and butter. The animals also provided much of the raw material for the craftsmen. Wool was the chief factor in clothing. Leather went into shoes and other garments, and it was also used to make drinking vessels. Many tools have been dug up for processing the wool and hides—spindle-whorls and loom-weights used in spinning and weaving; knives for skinning carcases, stone 'rubbers' for smoothing the hides, iron awls for piercing leather, and thick iron needles for sewing it. The Britons also used the horns, sinew, and gut of their animals, and made combs and pins out of the bones.

Besides keeping livestock, they ploughed the soil and raised crops. They ground the grain in hand-mills of Roman pattern, better than the type used outside the Empire. Bread was baked on stone discs, coming out in thin cakes rather than loaves.

To go back to our picture of the dark-age king or nobleman, we must see him as something between a Roman citizen and a barbarian. He usually had some Roman tastes —drinking wine, for instance—and a fondness for luxuries imported from overseas, which he paid for with surplus hides and other produce of his estates. He spoke a Celtic language that was an early form of Welsh, but he might well know some Latin too, and even read books in it. His life was often warlike. But the wars were fought in open country, and seldom troubled his household directly with sieges and raids. He might prefer to live in a place he could easily defend, like Dinas Powys. But as a rule he did not feel any need to fortify it on a grand scale. Here Cadbury Castle stands alone, an exception. That is one reason for believing that the man who lived there had a very special position and may well have been Arthur.

What can we say about religion and the arts?

The British kings and most of their subjects belonged to the Church. Christianity had become the faith of the Roman Empire while Britain was still under Rome's control. At first it did not sink very deep. But in the fifth and early sixth centuries a series of British missionaries converted the mass of their fellow-countrymen, and also the Irish, and some of the mixed tribes that lived in Scotland. The most famous was, of course, St. Patrick. But St. Ninian, St. Illtud, St. Cadoc, St. Sampson, and St. David also carried on a fruitful and civilising work that stretched from the Clyde to Brittany.

They and their Irish brethren created what is known as the Celtic Church. The reason for the name is that although these Christians never actually broke with the Church on the Continent, they were almost out of touch for a long while, and ran their affairs in a special style of their own.

All the principal churchmen of the British Isles were monks, and the Church was governed by abbots instead of bishops. The three chief religious centres of Arthur's Britain are said to have been Amesbury in Wiltshire, Glastonbury, and Llantwit Major in South Wales. None of these places was the seat of a bishop, but all three had big communities of monks.

This difference brought advantages and also drawbacks. The British monks were freer, and more democratic in their outlook, than priests on the Continent. Women were more respected, because, where monks were important, nuns were important too. There was more freedom of thought. Books which the Church tried to ban abroad could be read among the Celtic Christians. Various pagan ideas and myths stayed alive and passed into folklore—even into the stories of Arthur, those about the Grail, for instance.

Above: Remains of a dark-age helmet from Derbyshire. This is the iron frame; it enclosed a kind of cap which has rotted away. (PHOTO: J. A. COULTHARD—CITY MUSEUM, SHEFFIELD.) *Below:* 'Hanging bowl' of a type made by British craftsmen. This one was found in the early Saxon treasure at Sutton Hoo, and may be the work of a Briton employed by a Saxon king. (BRITISH MUSEUM)

But the monks despised worldly goods and tried to live as simply as possible. So the Church did not encourage the arts as much as in other countries. Arthur's Britons seem to have had very little painting or sculpture, except in the form of decoration. Their architecture was crude.

As we have seen, an art that did flourish was poetry, because the bards counted for so much at the kings' courts. Some of their verse has survived in four Welsh manuscripts. Little or none of it is quite as early as Arthur. The monk Gildas, writing in the 540s, does mention bards at a court in Wales. But their poems have been lost. The earliest complete poems that we have are the work of a group of bards in Rheged—roughly, Cumberland. The greatest were Taliesin and Aneirin. Another was Myrddin. (He was Geoffrey of Monmouth's original for Merlin, though he cannot have played the part in Arthur's adventures that Merlin does. If they met at all, Arthur was old and Myrddin a small boy.) The poems were meant to be recited aloud to an audience, with musical backing by a stringed instrument. Most are about the famous men of the time, praising their brave deeds and generosity, or lamenting their death.

Taliesin wandered. He is said to have begun his career at the court of Maelgwn, the king of Gwynedd, the same whose fortress is at Degannwy. A legend of Taliesin's first public performance tells how he arrived there as a boy, cast a spell on the king's bards so that they could only mumble, and then sang a riddling song making fun of their pretended wisdom. While the story cannot be altogether true, even apart from the magic in it, the image of Taliesin as an impudent teenage singer who shocked his elders comes through believably.

When Taliesin was older he moved to Rheged and settled down. His poems praise the north British kings who fought the Angles in Northumberland. In 'The Death Song of

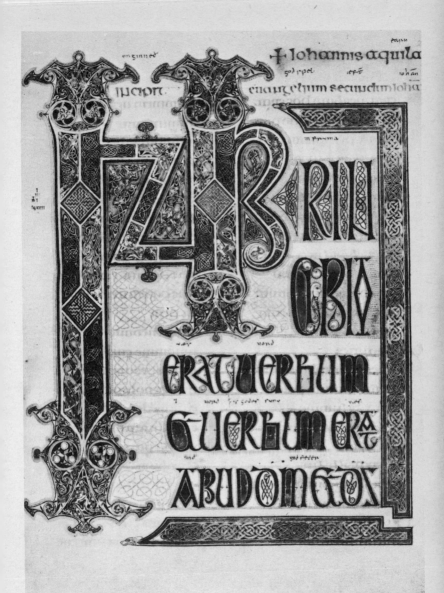

Page from the Lindisfarne Gospels (the opening of St. John in Latin, *In principio erat Verbum* . . .). The linear designs show how the decorative art of the Celtic Church influenced Anglo-Saxon writers. (BRITISH MUSEUM)

Owein' we get a sudden glimpse of enemy corpses slain by Owein, lying staring-eyed on the battlefield:

His keen-edged spears were like the wings of the dawn . . .
The host of broad England sleeps
With the light in their eyes.

Aneirin, too, sang of the northern wars. His masterpiece is *Gododdin*. In it is one of the oldest known references to Arthur by name, though only in passing, as the supreme warrior of Britain. *Gododdin* is a long poem of mourning for a band of 363 Britons who rode south from somewhere near Edinburgh to fight the Angles at 'Catraeth'—Catterick in Yorkshire—and were nearly all killed. Aneirin himself rode with them and was one of the few who escaped, 'because of my fine songs', he says. He portrays the gaily dressed warriors at their farewell banquet, drinking mead, listening to the minstrels, and going to church before they set off on the doomed expedition. They fight valiantly, but the enemy are too many for them:

The warriors arose together, together they met, together they attacked, with a single purpose; short were their lives, long the mourning left to their kinsmen. Seven times as many English they slew; in fight they made women widows, and many a mother with tears at her eyelids. . . . After the battle, may their souls get welcome in the land of heaven, the dwelling-place of plenty.

Aneirin's poem is the elegy of Arthur's Britain, going down nobly, yet nevertheless going down. But the long struggle was not in vain. The Britons had held out for so long that the Angles and Saxons who at last conquered were far more civilised than the ones who had first come over. While Aneirin lamented, St. Augustine's mission was

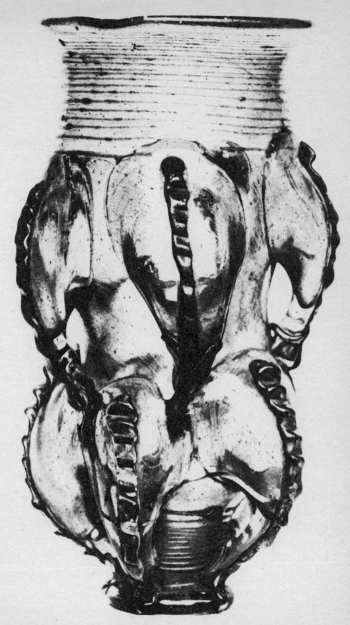

A glass claw-beaker, made in the early 6th century, and found at Castle Eden, Co. Durham. (BRITISH MUSEUM)

already at work in Kent. An England was beginning to take shape that would not be the deadly enemy portrayed by the bards. When it became a more peaceful country it was not a barbaric wilderness but the most advanced land of western Europe, enriching its life from the British and Roman heritage which Arthur had done so much to save. The descendants of Britons and Anglo-Saxons intermarried. Welsh princesses became queens of England. Today, Arthur's Britain is part of all of us.

10

HOW ARTHUR DID RETURN

IT IS TIME NOW TO TAKE another look at the Arthurian Legend—that marvellous daydream which grew so strangely from the traditions of the dark age. As you will remember, it was Sir Thomas Malory who put it into the form we know best. Before him no single author had gathered the medieval stories together, or told them in order as a series. Malory did this. In 1485 his work was edited and published by Caxton.

Caxton called the book *Morte d'Arthur*, The Death of Arthur, because he saw it as a tragedy. It held up a high ideal, but it closed with the Round Table ruined, and Arthur in his grave at Glastonbury. Malory, however, did mention the prophecy that the King would come back, and said many believed it. By 1485 more Englishmen than ever were wishing they could believe it. They were sick of disasters that had been going on for longer than anyone could recall—plagues and uprisings, foreign wars ending in defeat, civil wars killing tens of thousands, horrible crimes by rival kings and their followers.

Of course, it was too much to hope that Arthur would literally return from Avalon (wherever Avalon was). But if only—somehow or other—his peerless British kingdom could be reborn! And so strong was the impression of

Richard Harris as King Arthur in the film *Camelot*. (WARNER BROS.—
SEVEN ARTS)

something glorious that had once happened in Britain, and might again, that Malory's work was a new beginning. The Legend sprang into fresh life, and has gone on inspiring writers and artists ever since.

It might never have done this under its own power. But there was a special reason. In the same year as the *Morte d'Arthur* was published, Henry Tudor won the battle of Bosworth and became King Henry VII. Partly Welsh and proud of it, he marched from Wales to claim the crown under the standard of the Red Dragon, an emblem of Arthur's Britain in Geoffrey of Monmouth and earlier. Henry was an able ruler. Also, he was good at propaganda. He persuaded many of his subjects that he had fulfilled the prophecy. By the advent of a Welsh king descended from the Britons in Geoffrey's *History*, Arthur's realm actually was restored. The long reign of the Saxons, and the Normans after them, was over at last. Now the 'Briton' Henry VII would save the country. He would heal the wounds of civil war and bring in a golden age.

Henry named his eldest son Arthur and planned that he should become King Arthur II. The prince was christened at Winchester, which Malory said was Camelot. Unfortunately he died young. But the idea was kept up. When scholars protested that Geoffrey of Monmouth was a liar anyhow, Tudor supporters rallied to his defence. So he went on being read as serious history for another hundred years.

In the reign of Henry's granddaughter, Elizabeth I, the loyalists went further. They said a British prophet had fore-told her in person nearly a thousand years earlier. When she travelled, her hosts sometimes put on pageants with Arthurian scenes—a Lady of the Lake tableau, for instance, at Kenilworth Castle. Her astrologer John Dee started a notion that she had a right to rule over North America

Henry VII, a partly-Welsh king, who used the traditions of Arthur to strengthen his own claim to the throne. (NATIONAL PORTRAIT GALLERY)

Knight slaying dragon. An illustration in the first edition of Spenser's *Faerie Queene*. (RADIO TIMES HULTON PICTURE LIBRARY)

because Arthur's subjects had crossed the Atlantic long before the Spaniards. Elizabethan playwrights drew on Geoffrey for plots. Even Shakespeare, though he never wrote a play on Arthur, took King Lear and Cymbeline out of Geoffrey's book.

Edmund Spenser, next to Shakespeare the greatest poet of the age, carried the Tudors' claim to its dizziest height. In his long though unfinished *Faerie Queene*, dedicated to Elizabeth, he portrays Arthur as a young prince, riding through the land rescuing knights from perils on quests of their own. Merlin and other Malory characters cross the stage. Here, Spenser explains, is the story of Arthur's education in knightly qualities before he was king. (There was to have been a sequel about his reign, but it was never written.) The poet makes the events and people of the legendary world foreshadow his own time. He retells most of Geoffrey's *History*, saying in plain words that Elizabeth's realm is the kingdom of the Britons restored. Tudor England has a divine blessing and sacred mission, as Arthur has in the poem. Through its triumph over Philip of Spain, God will crush the powers of evil.

Elizabeth died in 1603. King James I tried to take over her glories for the House of Stuart. But he made himself too unpopular. The leading English poets of Stuart times, Milton and Dryden, both thought of writing on King Arthur. Milton, however, decided not to. Dryden only managed a not very good opera, *King Arthur*, just saved by Purcell's music. As once before, it looked as if no one had any more to say on the subject. But again its spell was too potent.

With the coming of the romantic writers of the nineteenth century, such as Sir Walter Scott, interest revived. Poets and novelists took the Legend up once more. So did artists. Most

Sir Galahad, a Victorian painting by G. F. Watts. Tennyson's *Idylls of the King* revived interest in Arthur and his court. (MANSELL COLLECTION)

of the best-known pictures of Arthurian scenes are by the Pre-Raphaelite school of painters and by Gustave Doré, working from the 1850s onward. For a while the most widely read of all versions of the Round Table adventures was Alfred Tennyson's in his *Idylls of the King*, a cycle of long poems which he was steadily adding to from 1855 into the 1870s.

Tennyson was Poet Laureate. He felt a deep respect for Queen Victoria and her husband, Prince Albert. After Albert's death in 1861 he dedicated the *Idylls* to his memory, and used them to voice his own beliefs about ideal monarchy and religion. In his day Tennyson was a best-seller. Modern readers seldom care much for the *Idylls*: if King Arthur interests them, they usually prefer to go back to Malory, or else turn to more recent authors. But while Tennyson may sound old-fashioned and priggish, he had a fine command of language, and some of the thoughts which he weaves into the Arthurian Legend are new to it.

His Arthur is King of Britain and also a symbolic figure. He stands for the human soul struggling against evil. The problems of his kingdom are the problems of life. When he crushes the heathen, when he clears the land of wild beasts, he is fighting the endless fight against the wickedness in human nature. Through the Round Table he tries to realise Christian values on earth. Here Tennyson makes a change of his own. Instead of the courtly love-affairs so popular with the romancers of the Middle Ages, he brings in the ideal of Christian marriage. King Arthur encourages his knights to have wives and set an example of model family life. There were hints of this idea in Malory and Spenser, but Tennyson takes it much further.

The message of his *Idylls* is not that a government inspired by religion will really work, or that spiritual ideals

The Vision of the Grail. A tapestry by William Morris, after a design by Edward Burne-Jones, the Pre-Raphaelite painter. (MANSELL COLLECTION)

can be practised for long in everyday life, but that we must keep trying. Arthur's attempt sets up a standard to aim at. He never achieves much more than that himself. His glory fades. Human faults undermine the Round Table. When Guinevere herself is unfaithful to her husband, the knights no longer take their marriage vows seriously. Most of their other principles go the same way.

Tennyson adds a second, less-obvious reason for Arthur's rule sliding downhill. The Quest of the Grail is a disaster too. The knights who seek it think they are in pursuit of the highest things. But what it actually does is to lure them away from their proper duties. Many are lost for ever. The new knights who take their place are lesser men.

When Arthur has been weakened in both these ways his subjects begin questioning his right to reign. They recall old doubts as to whose son he is, and whether he should be king at all. Tennyson seems to be suggesting that even the greatest hero or saint is liable to fail in the end, because it is never certain enough that he is in the right. Anyhow, Arthur's enemies rebel. He is wounded in the 'last weird dim battle of the west'. Sir Bedevere casts away Excalibur in one of the most famous passages of Tennyson's poetry, and the King disappears over the water in a boat. Yet we feel that the end is not the end. Arthur is immortal. His brave attempt is not a mere failure, but a pattern for others who may do better. There will be a Return. In the last line Sir Bedevere sees a new sunrise bringing a new year.

Tennyson's *Idylls* reached a public numbered in millions. They inspired plays, paintings, even an Arthur picture-series made by a most original photographer with live models. Other poets, such as Swinburne and Thomas Hardy, took up parts of the Legend which Tennyson had not treated fully. In Germany meanwhile, Richard Wagner had composed his

The dragon-slaying in Spenser again. A version by Morrell. (RADIO
TIMES HULTON PICTURE LIBRARY)

famous operas *Parsifal* (on the Grail) and *Tristan and Isolde.*

But writers and musicians were getting close to a point where they could not do much more with the romantic version. During the twentieth century the theme has taken a new turn. Several new turns, in fact. The change is due partly to the researches we have been looking at in this book. Little by little, fresh ideas have been seeping in. Writers no longer feel that they can handle the subject in the old way, and they no longer want to. They are aware now of the ancient traditions behind Geoffrey and Malory; aware, also, of the facts which are coming slowly into daylight.

In 1927 John Masefield—who became Poet Laureate like Tennyson—published a book of verse rehandling some of the stories of Arthur. Its title is *Midsummer Night.* Masefield's poems are fast-moving, easy to read, often with a brisk ballad-like effect. He mingles medieval romance and Welsh legend and historical fact in a fresh way, sometimes altering the familiar plots.

The 1950s brought a series of books and plays carrying this change further. Alfred Duggan, one of the best modern historical novelists, was first in the field. His *Conscience of the King* is a grimly comic dark-age adventure yarn, with Arthur seen through Saxon eyes as the leader of a terrifying cavalry force. R. C. Sherriff (best known as the author of *Journey's End*, a very successful play about the First World War) presented a rather different Arthur in another play called *The Long Sunset.* This shows how the last Roman officials in Britain might have tried to hand over power to native princes. Henry Treece's novel *The Great Captains* shows Arthur shockingly as a sinister fraud, owing most of his victories to followers such as Modred who have never been given the credit they deserve. After Treece, three women novelists gave their readers glimpses of dark-age Britain from other angles—Meriol Trevor, *The Last of Britain*; Bryher, *Ruan*; and Anya Seton, *Avalon*.

But the most important treatments of Arthur in recent fiction are two extreme cases. About 1960 Rosemary Sutcliff, up to then a writer of children's stories, became so fascinated with the history she had studied while writing them that she set to work on an adult novel depicting Arthur and his Britain as they might really have been. *Sword at Sunset* came out in 1963 and was a best-seller. Rosemary Sutcliff's picture of the British leader as a commander of mobile cavalry is very much as suggested in our own Chapter 3. She locates Mount Badon at Liddington. Her vivid account of the battle is based on advice from a professional soldier who worked out how it might have happened.

At the other extreme from Rosemary Sutcliff is T. H. White. A strange, lonely man with all sorts of rare knowledge about animals, outdoor sports, and many other topics, White scored a success in 1938 with *The Sword in the Stone*. This is a brilliant and funny version of Arthur's boyhood and his education by Merlin. Over a long stretch of time White wrote three more books retelling Malory in his own surprising manner. Having altered *The Sword in the Stone* to make it fit better with the rest, he brought out all four in 1958 under the title *The Once and Future King*. Again he won a big public. The stage and film musical *Camelot* was taken from this book.

White had no use for the sort of people who were trying to dig up a real Arthur or find out the historical truth. Still, he could not ignore them. To make his story work as he wished, he broke finally with all pretence that it was founded on history. Geoffrey of Monmouth, Chrétien de Troyes, and

143

Sir Lancelot comes to Arthur's court. Another scene from the film *Camelot*. (WARNER BROS.—SEVEN ARTS)

Malory certainly believed that their tales of Arthur were true in a way. Even Tennyson left the question in the air. But with T. H. White we move into a world that is right outside history as we know it. For him it is truer than history itself. He speaks of kings like Henry III as if *they* were imaginary and Arthur was real. Sometimes he deliberately turns the facts upside down. For example, he makes out the Celtic peoples like the Irish and Welsh to have been Arthur's enemies.

There is no need to set up onè author against another—to say that Rosemary Sutcliff is 'right' and T. H. White 'wrong', or the other way round. Both can be read and enjoyed. But it does look as if White's work will be left standing by itself. Any future stories, poems, or plays on this theme are likely to draw less on medieval legend, more on the realities of dark-age Britain, as these are steadily raised to the surface. Already we have been given a junior version of the Arthur of history by George Finkel in his story *Twilight Province*.

The Cadbury Castle excavations, beginning in 1966, aroused interest that led to TV programmes and to 'Arthurian' events in the annual Bath Festival. New societies have been formed to explore dark-age problems. Groups of scholars like the International Arthurian Society, who used to study the literature alone, are now taking far more interest in the facts behind it. The trend is plain. For imaginative writers as well as scientific investigators, the best hope of getting any more out of this national legend lies in an ever deeper knowledge of Britain—not just books, but the land of Britain itself, present and past: on the surface, and below.

The 'Round Table' at Winchester Castle. This existed in the Middle Ages, but its exact date is unknown. (PHOTO: SYDNEY W. NEWBERY)

11

THE MAP

THERE IS NO SUBSTITUTE FOR going to a place yourself. We will end our quest by taking a look at the Arthurian map of Britain, and picking out the places which are worth visiting—as part of the Legend, or as pointers towards the Fact, or as both at once.

The main drawback at present is that while we can pinpoint quite a number of places, there may be little to see when we get there. Most of the solid relics of Britain's dark age have been carried off to museums, or lie still buried in the earth, waiting to be dug up. Even the most picturesque yarns may lead us to nothing but a grass-covered earthwork, or a stone, or a stream like dozens of other streams.

But if the shortage of remains is a disappointment, it is also a challenge. Just because these dark-age scenes give so little away, they pose marvellous riddles. And anybody can try his hand at solving them. He can try piecing together the scraps of evidence—place-names, local legends, subtle clues in the lay of the land perhaps—that may guide archaeologists towards fresh treasures and further proofs. If he is very lucky he may be the one who opens up a new site by making the first tell-tale discoveries. The Camelot dig would never have started when it did if it hadn't been for Mrs. Harfield with her umbrella, poking bits of pottery out of the topsoil.

As we build up our map we should keep two questions in mind. Not only, 'What are the places where we can go and see something today?' but also, 'What are the places where we are at least on the trail of Arthur's Britain, and may catch a new glimpse of it tomorrow?'

Suppose we start at Tintagel Castle in Cornwall, where the Arthur of the Legend was born. As we saw, the castle was not built till long after the real Arthur, and there is no definite reason to believe that he ever came here. But at least the monastery existed in his time and belonged to his world. Also we should remember how the 'Tintagel' pottery used by the monks became one of the most precious clues for archaeologists. Tintagel is important even from the strict scientific point of view. Quite apart from which, its spell is too strong to break.

The village is a short distance inland from the cliffs along the Bristol Channel, and well above sea-level. Leaving the souvenir shops behind, we walk down through a valley with a stream in it. At the end the stream drops sharply to a cove, where the tide runs in and out over a broad beach. The huge headland with the castle ruins is on the left, almost cut off. With the aid of a guidebook we can climb all over its upper spaces, picking out the various parts of the ruin, and the scanty traces of the dark-age monastery.

There are hollows in the rock with names like 'Arthur's Chair', 'Arthur's Cups and Saucers'. Below, at beach level, a natural tunnel called Merlin's Cave pierces right through the base of the headland. As the tide rises, the waves sweep in from the western entry, and boil up to a roaring and magnificent turmoil in the semi-darkness midway.

After Tintagel the other Cornish sites may seem rather tame, if charming, as in the case of a pond where the Round Table is said to rise from the water if you watch for it on the

Tintagel Castle: part of the ruins in profile. At the base of the headland, on the right, is the entrance to Merlin's Cave. (PHOTO: CHARLES WOOLF)

right night. Down the coast is Padstow, with the neighbouring parish of Egloshayle and its small, battered hill-fort, which may be Kelliwic, Arthur's fortress in the early Welsh tales. Neither this nor Castle Dore has much to show but the remains of earthworks.

When we come to the cliffs at Land's End and look west towards the Isles of Scilly we are looking at a bigger puzzle. Today this is all an expanse of dangerous water, with reefs and fast currents. Legend, however, says that in Arthur's day the islands and rocks and mainland were all joined up, forming the lost land of Lyonesse. Tristram was born here. A famous tournament took place in Surluse, now under the Atlantic.

In Cornish tradition this drowned country is sometimes known as Lethowstow. Fishermen used to claim that their nets drew up bits of windows and masonry from the Seven Stones reef (where the tanker *Torrey Canyon* was wrecked in 1967 and polluted the beaches with her oil). The sea is supposed to have covered Lethowstow—or Lyonesse—in a single rush. The sole survivor was a man named Trevelyan, who jumped on horseback and rode madly just ahead of the waves. The arms of the Trevelyan family portray a horse coming out of water.

Most of this talk is fancy, but not all of it. There was a small but real Lyonesse in and around the Scillies. A Roman writer, not so very long before Arthur, speaks of a single 'Isle' of Scilly. Since then the sea has gradually broken this up into the cluster of little islands we know. But ancient stone walls can be seen on what is now the sea-bed between them. The floors of British huts and graves have been found below the modern high-water mark, with Roman pottery and jewellery, proving that Britons were living there well into the Christian era.

The new science of underwater archaeology may soon tell us more. So far, divers have been more interested in the wrecks of treasure ships. But already a small expedition—near the islets of Great and Little Arthur!—has proved that there is more of the real Lyonesse among the Scillies, waiting to be explored.

Coming back to the Cornish mainland, we can cross the bleak expanses of Bodmin Moor and notice natural rock-features with names like 'Arthur's Hall'. The River Camel is one of the supposed scenes of the King's last battle with Modred, and Dozmary Pool is one of the places where Sir Bedevere threw away Excalibur. Beside the Camel is Arthur's Tomb, a stone slab.

Devonshire gives far less. In Somerset the two chief Arthurian places are, of course, Glastonbury and Cadbury Castle, which we already know. The large-scale Ordnance Survey map shows remnants of an old raised track running from one to the other, 'King Arthur's Hunting Causeway'. Whatever its real age, there may be more to find out about this track.

Beside the Bristol Channel is Dunster. Near here Arthur met St. Carannog and chased the serpent. Dunster Castle, however, is more recent by many centuries. Farther up the coast is Brent Knoll, a hill standing by itself. It used to belong to Glastonbury Abbey. The monks said it was given to the Abbey by Arthur. Brent Knoll is known to have been inhabited in early times, but it has not yet been fully studied.

The hill drew some interest in 1966, when Leslie Alcock's team at Cadbury Castle dug up the pottery proving that Cadbury had been occupied in the dark ages. It was pointed out that the same kind of ware had now been found on three hills—Cadbury, Glastonbury Tor, and Dinas Powys across the Bristol Channel—and that these lay almost along a straight line, with flat country and the sea between. Brent Knoll is not far off the same line, and can be seen both from the Tor and from Dinas Powys. Could the four hills have been linked by some sort of signalling system—beacons perhaps—so that messages could pass quickly between Arthur and his allies in Wales? No evidence has turned up yet. But if dark-age occupation were to be proved at Brent Knoll as well as the other three hills, this would be exciting.

We may now jump seventy miles to Liddington Castle, just south of Swindon, one of the best candidates for Mount Badon. It is a vast hill-fort at the end of the ridgeway, rising nine hundred feet above sea-level, with the village of Badbury close by. The ancient banks tower up sharply around the central enclosure, and the ditches are deep. Liddington is a splendid site and seems to be in the right area for a great victory at the right time. But it must not be forgotten that some prefer to locate Mount Badon at Badbury Rings, the hill-fort in Dorset, or at Bath.

After so much grass and guesswork we may like to visit Winchester, the old capital of England and Malory's Camelot. The King Arthur of romance is the figure whom this city recalls. Today its cathedral and other buildings can still take us back to the Middle Ages. On a wall inside the castle hangs the 'Round Table' itself—a genuine antique, though hardly antique enough to be the original! Caxton, introducing his edition of Malory, mentions this mighty wooden disc. The Table is divided into painted segments. It looks rather like a giant dart-board. Places are marked on it for the King and his chief knights.

In 1486 Henry VII brought his son to Winchester Cathedral to be christened Arthur, as part of his plan to convince England that an age of glory had returned. At Winchester too, in the College, a manuscript of Malory's

View of the Isles of Scilly, looking over St. Martin's. Most of the Scillies were once joined together. The land between, now submerged, is the original Lyonesse. (AEROFILMS LTD.)

writings was discovered in 1934. It gave scholars many new insights into the way Sir Thomas worked.

If the medieval versions of Arthur interest us we can pass from Winchester to Caerleon-upon-Usk, where Geoffrey of Monmouth placed his court. Here it is plain how much the story changed between Geoffrey and Malory, and how much nearer Geoffrey was to the facts, in spite of all his nonsense. At Caerleon, the Legion City, there is not much that dates from the Middle Ages. But the Roman remains—excavated in the 1920s—stare us in the face. Plenty of the amphitheatre is still left. The foundations of the soldiers' quarters cover acres of ground, all very straight and square and precise. Caerleon has a museum with Roman objects dug up on the site. Somewhere in the neighbourhood there is said to be another cave like the Cadbury one, where several of Arthur's knights lie asleep till they are needed.

Geoffrey of Monmouth does not take us any farther north (at least, not usefully). But Nennius, the earlier Welshman who gives that odd list of Arthur's battles, has two even odder paragraphs about what he calls 'marvels', in Herefordshire and Wales. One is at Archenfield:

> There is a burial mound near a spring which is known as Licat Anir, and the name of the man who is buried in the mound is Anir. He was the son of Arthur the soldier, and Arthur himself killed him there and buried him. And when men come to measure the length of the mound, they find it sometimes six feet, sometimes nine, sometimes twelve, and sometimes fifteen. Whatever length you find it at one time, you will find it different at another, and I myself have proved this to be true.

Alas, nobody knows exactly where the elastic grave is. Anyone who finds it and confirms the story will have made a real discovery.

Dozmary Pool, Cornwall. According to local legend Excalibur is at the bottom. (PHOTO: CHARLES WOOLF)

Nennius's second Arthurian marvel is in Builth, a district of Brecknockshire:

There is a heap of stones, and on the top of the heap one stone bearing the footprint of a dog. When they hunted the boar Troit, Cabal which was the dog of Arthur the soldier, put his foot on that stone and marked it; and Arthur afterwards piled up a heap of stones and that stone on top, on which was the dog's footprint, and called it Carn Cabal. And men will come and carry away that stone for a day and a night, and the next morning there it is back again on its heap.

Arthur's great boar-hunt is described in the Welsh tale *Culhwch and Olwen*. But again the spot is uncertain.

From here on, the map is largely a scatter of hazy folk-lore. More caves, with more sleeping knights in them, are said to exist in Glamorgan and Carmarthen, and in Caernarvon near Snowdon. Another cave in this third county, by Marchlyn Mawr, has Arthur's treasure in it. (Dreadful things will happen to you if you touch it.) Anglesey has yet another cave, where Arthur sheltered during one of his wars.

Besides the caves, Wales has other features—rock formations, standing stones, and so forth—with Arthurian names or legends attached to them. Here is a list, which is probably far from complete.

BRECKNOCKSHIRE
Arthur's Chair, between two peaks.
Arthur's Hill-top.
Arthur's Table.

GLAMORGAN
Arthur's Stone.
Guinevere's Monument (at Llaniltern).

Arthur's seat, near Edinburgh. (PHOTO: G. J. BAKKER)

CARMARTHEN
Arthur's Pot (a rock which Merlin shaped for cooking).

MERIONETH
Caergai, the home of Kay, beside Lake Bala, where the Dee rises.
Llyn Barfog, where Arthur killed a monster, and his horse left a hoofprint on the rock.

CAERNARVON
The River of Arthur's Kitchen.
Cairns of Arthur and Tristram.
Dinas Emrys, Ambrosius's hill-fort in Snowdonia (see Chapter 6).

ANGLESEY
Arthur's Quoit.
The Round Table (a rock formation).

DENBIGH
The Round Table (another rock formation).

FLINTSHIRE
Arthur's Hill.

Northern England is not so rich. However, the story of the slumbering King, or knights, turns up again at Alderley Edge in Cheshire, Threlkeld in Cumberland, and The Sneep in Durham. Near Sewingshields, in Northumberland, is a mass of rock called King's Crags, with an Arthur's Chair in it. He sat here and tossed a boulder at Guinevere on Queen's Crags. Over in the Cumberland border country are another natural Round Table and a hill or two. Near Birdoswald on

Arthur's Quoit in Cornwall—one of several ancient stone structures which are connected with him in legend, but are actually much earlier. (PHOTO: EDWIN SMITH)

Hadrian's Wall is the Roman fort of Camboglanna, which some think is Camlann, the scene of Arthur's last battle.

It may be a surprise to learn that Scotland has more of these sites than northern England. Arthur's Seat, the hill close by Edinburgh, is the best known. Besides this, there is another cave where Arthur lies sleeping, in the Eildon Hills south of Melrose. A Ben Arthur rises among the mountains of Dumbarton. Lanark has Arthur's Fountain; Stirling, Arthur's Oven and an earthwork Round Table; Peebles, Merlin's Grave; Angus, Arthur's Fold and Arthur's Stone and another Arthur's Seat. Vague bits of folklore about the King, Guinevere, and Modred take us as far as Perth and Kincardine.

The names with 'Arthur' in them often refer to natural features rather than to anything built by men. 'Arthur' in this folklore sense is spread over Britain more widely than anybody else except the Devil. Probably the list does not give us much history. In fact, Arthur names turn up across the Channel in Brittany, where he is not likely ever to have lived. There is even one in the sky. Some Cornishmen call the constellation of the Great Bear 'Arthur's Wain'. This doesn't prove that the King was an astronaut.

But the map is interesting in at least one way. The names and legends come in clusters. They are not spread evenly. We find them in Cornwall, then hardly at all in Devon, then again in Somerset. We find them in South Wales and North Wales, but much less in central Wales. Possibly, these groupings may hint at which areas were the most important in Arthur's time. Archaeology already seems to have shown that this is so in the West Country. Dark-age remains are more plentiful in Cornwall and Somerset than they are in Devon. The field is wide open for the explorer who wants to try fitting clues together in other parts of Britain.

APPENDIX I

THE MOST
IMPORTANT
CHARACTERS

AMBROSIUS

King of Britain before Uther, his brother. Historically, Ambrosius Aurelianus, a leader of British resistance against the Saxons. In Welsh tradition, 'Emrys'—perhaps the lord of Dinas Emrys in Snowdonia, a hill-fort known to have been occupied by a prominent chieftain of the fifth century.

ARTHUR

In reality a British war-leader against the Saxons early in the sixth century, who won the battle of Mount Badon and checked the invasion. In legend, King of Britain and conqueror of many countries beyond the sea. Son of Uther and Ygerne. Born at Tintagel. Brought up by Sir Ector. Becomes king by drawing the sword from the stone, and overthrows many enemies. Marries Guinevere. Founds the Knights of the Round Table. Reigns at Camelot (Cadbury Castle?). Is recalled from an overseas campaign by Modred's revolt. Mortally wounded at Camlann and taken to the Isle of Avalon. Buried at Glastonbury Abbey; or still alive, perhaps sleeping in a cave in Cadbury Castle.

BEDEVERE or BEDIVERE

A knight who attends Arthur after Camlann and throws away Excalibur. Not important in the later stories, but more so in Geoffrey of Monmouth, and mentioned in early Welsh poetry as 'Bedwyr'. Probably an officer of the real Arthur.

BORS

One of the knights most successful in the Grail Quest. Goes to Sarras with Galahad and Percivale. Supports Lancelot in his quarrel with Arthur. Dies in the Holy Land fighting Saracens.

ELAINE

The Maid of Astolat. A young woman who falls hopelessly in love with Lancelot, and dies. Her body is carried down the river in a boat and seen by the court. In some versions she is the same as the Elaine of Carbonek who is the mother of Galahad.

GALAHAD

Son of Lancelot by Princess Elaine of Carbonek. The last descendant of Joseph of Arimathea, who brought the Grail to Britain. Sits in the *Siege Perilous*. Pure of heart and invincible, he achieves the Grail Quest and dies in Sarras.

GARETH

Youngest son of King Lot of Orkney. Serves in the kitchen under Sir Kay. Killed by Lancelot during his rescue of Guinevere.

GAWAIN

Eldest son of King Lot of Orkney. Becomes enemy of Lancelot because of the killing of his brother Gareth. Dies at Dover during the final war. Is the hero of the story of the Green Knight, and several others not told by Malory. The same person as an early Welsh hero called Gwalchmei, the 'Hawk of May'.

GUINEVERE

Daughter of a West Country king. Marries Arthur and presides with him over his court, but is unfaithful with Lancelot, who saves her from burning at the stake. Retires to a convent after the battle of Camlann. Buried at Glastonbury.

ISEULT

Daughter of the King of Ireland. Marries King Mark of Cornwall. She and Tristram are lifelong lovers, partly because of their accidentally drinking a love potion. They live together for a time as Lancelot's guests at his castle, Joyous Gard.

KAY

Son of Ector, Arthur's foster-father. Becomes Arthur's seneschal or steward. Like Bedevere, more important in earlier than later stories. Appears as 'Kei' in very early Welsh poetry. Probably an officer of the real Arthur.

LANCELOT OF THE LAKE

Son of King Ban of Benwick. The most splendid and chivalrous of the knights in the romances, but also the lover of Guinevere, and hence unworthy to attain the full vision of the Grail, though his son Galahad does. Besieged by Arthur in his castle Joyous Gard after saving the Queen from burning. Withdraws to France and arrives home too late to help Arthur at Camlann. Dies in a hermitage at Glastonbury.

LOT

King of Orkney. Marries Margawse, Ygerne's sister (or daughter, in some versions). Their sons include Gawain, Aggravayne, and Gareth. In some accounts Lot's wife is not Margawse but Anne, a sister of Arthur.

MAELGWN

King of Gwynedd in North Wales. The poet Taliesin first appears at his court as a boy, with a riddling song which puzzles the bards. Maelgwn was certainly a real king, who died about 547. His citadel was at Degannwy beside the Conway.

MARK

King of Cornwall, husband of Iseult. Tries to kill his nephew Tristram, and plots against various other knights. The hall discovered at Castle Dore may have been his.

MELLYAGRAUNCE or MELEAGANT

A nobleman who detains Guinevere in his castle, from which she is saved by Lancelot. In the oldest version he is 'King Melwas of Somerset' with a stronghold at Glastonbury, the probable traces of which have been discovered on the Tor.

MERLIN

Prophet and wizard. Said to have placed Stonehenge, by magic, on its present site. Guides Arthur in his youth and the early part of his reign. Imprisoned in a cave by the sorceress Nimue. Merlin is sometimes connected with the Grail. He appears first in the account by Geoffrey of Monmouth, who, however, based the character partly on an actual poet of the sixth century.

MODRED or MORDRED

The arch-villain. A son of Arthur's sister Anne, or of Margawse (see Lot). According to rumour, Arthur himself was Modred's true father. Modred sows discord for his own ends. While Arthur campaigns overseas he is left as regent, and revolts. The King returns; the battle of Camlann is fatal to them both, and to the Round Table. Modred figures in early Welsh writings as 'Medraut', an enemy of Arthur, and was probably a real person.

MORGAN LE FAY

Arthur's half-sister, the daughter of Ygerne by her first husband. Becomes a witch and troubles the kingdom with magic and plots.

NIMUE, NYNEVE, or (in Tennyson) VIVIEN

The Lady of the Lake. Entraps Merlin in a cave. However, her magic is generally helpful to Arthur, and she marries Pelleas, one of his knights. Said to have escorted the King to Avalon. (Tennyson makes the Vivien who entraps Merlin a different person from the Lady of the Lake.)

PALOMIDES

A Saracen knight, the unsuccessful rival of Tristram for the love of Iseult. After many encounters they are reconciled and Palomides becomes a Christian. Takes up the hunt of the Questing Beast after Pellinore.

PELLINORE

A local king, the senior member of the Round Table. Hunts the Questing Beast.

PERCIVALE

One of the chief seekers in the early Grail stories, especially the German *Parzival*. In Malory he is Pellinore's son, goes to Sarras with Galahad, sees the Grail, and dies without coming back.

TALIESIN

A poet of northern Britain. In Geoffrey of Monmouth's poem *The Life of Merlin* he is said to have escorted Arthur to Avalon. Began his career at the court of Maelgwn.

TRISTRAM or TRISTAN

Son of King Melyodas of Lyonesse. A great warrior and skilled musician. By killing the Irish champion Marhaus he saves his uncle Mark, King of Cornwall, from paying a tribute. Is the lifelong lover of the Irish princess Iseult, whom, however, he has to bring to Cornwall as Mark's bride. Later marries Isolde of Brittany, but remains loyal to Iseult. In some versions Isolde jealously brings about his death by a trick; in others he is stabbed by Mark. He can be traced back through Welsh legend, and is probably the British nobleman Drustans or Drustanus, whose memorial stone stands near Fowey in Cornwall. But, if so, the legends seem to have altered his parentage and relation with Mark.

UTHER

Called the Pendragon. King of Britain after his brother Ambrosius and before Arthur. Father of Arthur, and first owner of the Round Table.

VIVIEN

See Nimue.

YGERNE

Wife of the Duke of Cornwall. By him, the mother of Morgan le Fay. By Uther, her second husband, the mother of Arthur.

SOME SUGGESTED BOOKS

THESE ARE ONLY A FEW OUT of hundreds. You can find a longer reading list in the second of them, which covers much the same ground as ALL ABOUT KING ARTHUR but in far greater detail, with chapters on the various digs by the archaeologists who directed them.

The third book on this list gives a fuller account of the stories, with less on the history. I leave most of the others to speak for themselves.

Leslie Alcock, BY SOUTH CADBURY IS THAT CAMELOT ... Thames & Hudson, 1972.

Geoffrey Ashe (editor), THE QUEST FOR ARTHUR'S BRITAIN. Pall Mall Press, 1968. Paladin paperback, 1971.

R. W. Barber, ARTHUR OF ALBION. Barrie & Rockliff, 1961.

G. E. Daniel (editor), MYTH OR LEGEND? Bell, 1955.

George Finkel, TWILIGHT PROVINCE. Angus & Robertson, 1967.

Geoffrey of Monmouth, HISTORY OF THE KINGS OF BRITAIN. Translated from the Latin by Lewis Thorpe. Penguin Books, 1966.

THE MABINOGION. Translated from the Welsh by Gwyn and Thomas Jones. Dent, 1949.

Sir Thomas Malory, LE MORTE D'ARTHUR. Modern English version by Keith Baines, Mentor Classics (New American Library, New York), 1962. (This is by far the easiest reading. But of course there are many reprints of Malory's original, and Caxton's edition of it, in fifteenth-century English.)

Rosemary Sutcliff, SWORD AT SUNSET. Hodder & Stoughton, 1963.

Alfred Tennyson, THE IDYLLS OF THE KING. In any complete edition of Tennyson's poems. (Some editions do not include them all.)

T. H. White, THE SWORD IN THE STONE. Collins, 1938.

    THE ONCE AND FUTURE KING. Collins, 1958. (This includes THE SWORD IN THE STONE, but in a rewritten form which most people think is not so good.)

INDEX

INDEX REFERENCES FOR ILLUSTRATIONS

If you would like to receive a newsletter

telling you about our new children's books,

fill in the coupon with your name and address

and send it to:

Gillian Osband
Transworld Publishers Ltd.,
57–58 Uxbridge Road,
Ealing, London, W5

NAME ....

ADDRESS ....

....

....

CHILDRENS NEWSLETTER

IF YOU HAVE ENJOYED THIS BOOK YOU MAY ALSO LIKE THESE:

THE STORY OF BRITAIN
by R. J. Unstead   30p
Series   Carousel Non-Fiction

A country is forged by its history, the battles and intrigues of by-gone ages laying the foundations of today. From its beginnings as an island to the end of the Second World War, this series is the record of the men and women who played a role in shaping the character of England now. It traces the emergence of England as a nation.

EVERYDAY LIFE IN THE VIKING AGE
by Jacqueline Simpson   30p
552 54011 0   Carousel Non-Fiction

The Vikings were not merely plunderers and marauders, but also a civilised people with a culture of their own—as recent excavations have shown. Jacqueline Simpson provides a full and fascinating account of their way of life covering their domestic life as well as their better-known overseas adventures.

PARADE OF HORSES
by Vian Smith   30p
552 54022 6

This is the book for all who love horses. In his affectionate journey through the world of horses, Vian Smith tells of farm-horses and steeplechasers, circus horses, and the breeds which have disappeared over the years such as the fire and funeral pairs. Included are eight pages of photographs, and numerous drawings of different horses.

20TH CENTURY DISCOVERY: THE PLANETS
by Isaac Asimov 25p
552 54013 7 Carousel Non-Fiction

Dr. Asimov's books recount the major events of scientific discovery in this century: how the atom has been investigated and its power harnessed; how delicate the balance of nature is: and how, through his examination of the structure of life, man may have come close to the artifical creation of life itself; how the development of different telescopes has enabled man to observe the stars and planets, how he has calculated their age and distance, and how the development of space travel has affected our knowledge of the Universe.

Illustrated with photographs.

THE BOOK OF EXPERIMENTS
by Leonard de Vries 30p
552 54020 X

Would you like to become an inventor? This book will show you how. Would you like to experience the adventure of scientific discovery in your own home? This book offers 150 such experiments which can be done safely and at little or no cost—for example, with nails you can make either a piano or an electric motor. Many equally amazing discoveries await the reader of this book.

All these books are available at your bookshop or newsagent or can be ordered direct from **TRANSWORLD PUBLISHERS**. Just tick the titles you want and fill in the form below.

....

TRANSWORLD PUBLISHERS. Cash Sales Department, P.O. Box 11, Falmouth, Cornwall.

Please send cheque or postal order—no currency, and allow 6p per book to cover the cost of postage and packing.

NAME ....

ADDRESS..

(MAY/73)..